GLIMPSES AND IMPRESSIONS OF KIERKEGAARD

By Dr. T. H. Croxall

KIERKEGAARD COMMENTARY
MEDITATIONS FROM KIERKEGAARD

SØREN KIERKEGAARD

From a statuette by Louis Hasselriis in the Fredericksburg Museum

GLIMPSES AND IMPRESSIONS OF KIERKEGAARD

Selected and Translated by
T. H. CROXALL
D.D. et B.Mus.(Oxon.), F.R.C.O.

JAMES NISBET & CO. LTD.
DIGSWELL PLACE

Published by
James Nisbet and Company Limited
Digswell Place, Welwyn, Herts.

First published 1959

Made and printed in Great Britain by
William Clowes and Sons Ltd
London and Beccles

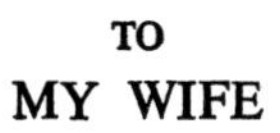

TO

MY WIFE

FOREWORD

Carl Weltzer, certainly one of the most painstaking and erudite of Kierkegaard interpreters, says, 'Henriette Lund's and H. Brøchner's *Recollections* are of abiding value. The material they contain seems to be presented without any sort of bias. They are pure narrations. True, Henriette Lund has not escaped letting her enthusiasm for her Uncle Søren find expression in a comparison—more beautiful than convincing—between Søren Kierkegaard and Prince Hamlet, where "resolution red as dawn" in Kierkegaard's attack on the Church, yields to "pale reflexion".[1] He is rather the knight of her childhood than "The Exception".[2] Yet she does also in one place report the disparaging words of her father—"that fantastic person!"[3]

'As a source for the understanding of Kierkegaard in his relationship with other people, Henriette Lund's memoirs stand in the first rank.'[4]

I am sure Weltzer is right. Brøchner's *Recollections*, translated in Part I of this book, and the excerpts from Henriette's in Part II give an agreeable and authentic picture of the great Søren Kierkegaard. And they are contemporary. They entirely dispel the idea of Kierkegaard as 'the melancholy Dane'. He is not 'melancholy' in our English sense of the word. One side of his nature was introspective and brooding,[5] but the world saw a gay and vivacious personality.

Part III of this book deals with Kierkegaard's death, and the vexed question of the attack on the Church connected with it. The matter is often painful and puzzling, and the documents (which have never appeared in English before, except for some very small scraps) may bring to those interested both clarification and comfort. Mixed up with the affair, too, is Søren's attitude to his brother, and his refusal to see Peter even on his death bed. In dealing with this I have been led to investigate the characters of the two men, again giving

[1] See extract 17 in Henriette Lund's *Recollections*.

[2] This is what Søren Kierkegaard constantly calls himself.

[3] See extract 11. According to Henriette, the mother too joined in this view. Henriette also disagrees with S.K.'s attitude towards women's education, and towards Grundtvig. See extracts 14 and 18.

[4] Carl Weltzer, *Peter & Søren Kierkegaard*, I, p. 8.

[5] The word often translated melancholy is *Tungsind*. Occasionally this word is equated, even in Danish, with melancholy, but in the Greek sense of 'passionate', 'mad' (See Plato *Republic*, 573, Aristotle *Ethics*, VII, 10.3) not in our English sense of gloom and depression. Rather, *Tungsind* means, as I say above, introspective and brooding. But even 'broodiness' is only one side of Kierkegaard's nature.

documents new to English readers. Here again, though there are no doubt things to regret, we gain clarification and understanding. The two had more in common than they thought. And were it not that they (and perhaps especially Søren) allowed personal feelings to enter so strongly into their differences of opinion—in a way the English on the whole do not—they might have been more in accord, and the rift between them not so great.

T. H. CROXALL

ACKNOWLEDGEMENTS

I express my deep gratitude to my wife and to Mrs. Evelyn Jones for typing the sheets. To the former's interest and advice I ever owe much. And I am grateful to Frøken Kirsten Bruun for advice on some things which only a Dane could know.

CONTENTS

PART I

HANS BRØCHNER

PART II

HENRIETTE LUND'S RECOLLECTIONS OF KIERKEGAARD

PART III

KIERKEGAARD'S DEATH AND LAST STRUGGLE WITH THE CHURCH

NOTE ON REFERENCES TO KIERKEGAARD'S WRITINGS

A letter in the middle of a reference (e.g. II, C, 24) indicates the latest edition of the *Papirer* and the last figure, whether in the Danish original or the English translation (*Dru's Journals*), indicates not a page, but the number of the entry. A reference with no letter in the middle (e.g. II, p. 24) indicates that it is from the *Værker*, and the last figure refers to a page.

The letters *E.P.* denote the first edition of the *Papirer* by Barfod, which are, entitled *Efterladte Papirer*.

In the quotations the English translation, if any, is given first, followed by the corresponding Danish reference.

The numbering in the Brøchner *Recollections* is Brøchner's own.

A SHORT BIOGRAPHY OF SØREN AABY KIERKEGAARD

Søren Aaby Kierkegaard was born at Copenhagen on 5 May 1813, and died there on 11 November 1855. Apart from four brief visits to Berlin, one visit to Jutland, one to Gilleleje, and tours in the neighbourhood of Copenhagen, Kierkegaard, like Socrates, did not leave his native city. His father, Michael Pedersen Kierkegaard, was born in December 1756 at Sæding in West Jutland. At the age of eleven, Michael's uncle fetched him to Copenhagen to help in his hosiery business there. In due course Michael set up a similar business on his own, and was so successful that at the age of forty he retired a very rich man. He had seven children, of whom Søren was the last, born when his father was fifty-seven and his mother forty-five. After his retirement Michael occupied himself with philosophy and theology, achieving remarkable success therein. He possessed great dialectical powers, and also an 'almighty imagination', both of which qualities Søren inherited. The mother was an 'even, simple character', but the father was just the opposite. Deeply religious, but extremely introspective and brooding, his dominating personality shrouded the home with an atmosphere of severity and rigour, not to say gloom, giving the impression that Christianity can never make a man happy. Nevertheless as a child Søren idolized his father.

At one time the family attended the meetings of the Moravian Brothers; but when Mynster (whom we shall meet in these pages), later a bishop, brought new life to the Danish church, Michael betook himself to him, and Mynster became his father-confessor. Søren retained a great deference towards Mynster; though, at the end, he attacked him bitterly.

At school Søren was not thought to be outstanding, though on leaving school in 1830, his headmaster gave him a good recommendation to the University; suggesting, however, that the boy was apt to dabble in many things, not being sufficiently pertinacious and deep at any.

Strange as it seems to us, Søren was at the University for ten years (1830–40). He reacted against his father's conception of Christanity, and though he was supposed to be studying theology, he soon subordinated this to the study of Romanticism, Folklore and Philosophy; such figures as Faust, Don Juan, and the Wandering Jew being his special studies. He was a member of the Student's

Union, where he gave some telling speeches. He also wrote good newspaper articles. Though, in fact, all these things were good for him and enriched his authorship, his father and brother felt them to be wrong. In 1835 therefore the father sent him on holiday to Gilleleje, and while there he took stock of himself, knowing that he needed an idea to live for, and that Christianity was his 'radical cure'. He resolved to take that cure, but when he was back in the University again, he immediately broke that resolution. He associated with bad company, and sowed wild oats, perhaps influenced by two discoveries. These were (1) that his father, as an eight-year-old shepherd boy out on the Jutland heath, had stood up and cursed God for his servile lot which made him suffer hardship, hunger, cold, and exhaustion; and (2) that his father had married his mother under compulsion, she being with child by him before they were married. Søren's idol had crashed: things went with him from bad to worse.

At last, perhaps in the winter term of 1835, he left home like a prodigal son. He contracted debts which his father paid—so large that on 1 September 1837, his father gave him a fixed allowance instead of paying debts *ad hoc*—and generally lived an extravagant and wild life. Yet his condition, if undisciplined, was wistful. On 22 April 1838 he wrote, 'If Christ is to come and make His abode with me, it must be, as the heading to today's Gospel-reading Almanac says, "Christ comes in through closed doors".'[1] And then, on 19 May, a month later, he records a sudden change. He speaks of an 'indescribable joy' which seized him that day; in other words, he experienced a religious conversion. A month later still, he was at Confession and Holy Communion again. Reconciled to his father, he now returned home; alas, not long before his father died. That death affected Søren profoundly. He returned, as his father had wished, to his theological studies, sat for his final examination in theology, and did well.

Meanwhile, in 1837, he had met a young girl named Regine Olsen, with whom he straightway fell in love. She was then only fourteen and a half years old, and he twenty-three. He did nothing, however, as yet. When his theological examinations were all over, he took a journey to Sæding, his father's birthplace (it was in July and August 1840), apparently determined that on his return he would propose marriage to Regine, who was then nearly eighteen; and so he did. She accepted, and they became engaged on 10 September 1840. The following November he entered the Pastoral Seminarium, a kind of theological college for the training of clergy. In fact, however, Kierkegaard never was ordained.

[1] *Journals*, 196 (II, A, 730).

But no sooner had he got engaged than he felt it a mistake. He could not, he thought, be an ideal husband, and less he would not be for Regine's sake. He felt himself to be, in many ways, what he called an 'Exception'. He had inherited his father's tendency to introspective broodiness, though, as these pages will abundantly show, he concealed it, and showed a pleasanter side to the world. He knew his father's sins, which he felt tainted the family. He had a 'thorn in the flesh' as he calls it, whatever it was; some 'misrelationship between soul and body', a 'fundamental injury', a 'spot'. He had sown his wild oats, and there is even talk of a sexual fall, though this is not proven. He had been trained by his father in a sombre theology; the father evidently designating him for the priesthood, perhaps as a sort of atonement-offering for his own sins. We read too of a 'silent despair' in which his father once said he moved. But over and above all, there is a secret we cannot penetrate, and which Kierkegaard has been at pains to conceal from the world. In my judgement we ought not to try to penetrate that secret.

So the engagement must, he felt, be brought to an end. But how? To cast Regine off would be to betray her. She must be made to cast *him* off. So he set to work to convince her that he was a scoundrel who had never loved her, though in fact the opposite was the case. In the middle of all the distress that this caused them, he was yet writing his thesis, entitled 'The Concept of Irony', for the higher degree of M.A. This thesis he publicly defended with success on 29 September 1841. Then on 11 October, when neither he nor Regine could hold out longer, she let him go. As an old lady Regine recorded that they 'parted without bitterness'. She said, 'You are now free, do not come to see me any more.'

In the Introduction to Part III below, and especially in Section 6 of that Part, more is said about this engagement; and some moving letters from Regine are adduced. The experience of it set a flame of genius alight in Kierkegaard, and deepened his religion. Indeed he always regarded it as a religious experience; an experience too that set him on his path of authorship. It would not do for us all to be the Exception like Kierkegaard; indeed that were impossible. But his Christianity is there for us all to profit by; and if this came to him through his particular experiences, we must accept the fact and be grateful. Kierkegaard was weak in body, often sick in mind—both things he fully recognized—but, as he rightly says, he was never sick in spirit; and it is this fact that makes him for ever great. He could psycho-analyse (without jargon) his own condition with great penetration. And, unlike many patients, he conquered his condition and found the cure.

But further sufferings were to follow. A comic paper called the *Corsair* founded in 1840, made it its business to attack and poke fun at people of distinction. Many thought this a public scandal; though nowadays we should not take nearly so much notice. Kierkegaard tells us that he felt moved of God to oppose it. He asked to be taken note of in the *Corsair*; and on 2 January 1846 he was. Thereupon he was able to make slashing replies and exposures. He got more, however, than he bargained for. The attacks continued for some months, but they led to public ridicule which endured for more than two years. This ridicule was carried to incredible lengths. His ungainly figure, his trousers, his broken engagement, were all made fun of. Yet, just because of all this, he determined not to leave Copenhagen. He had formerly contemplated getting ordained and taking a living as a country priest. Hence his term at the Pastoral Seminarium. Now he finally gave that up. He would stand his ground. On 24 January 1847 he wrote, 'God be praised that all this attack of the mob came upon me. I have had time to discover and be assured that it would have been depressing to live in a country parsonage in order to become a penitent in seclusion and forgetfulness. Now I stand as never before steadfast in my place' (*Papirer*, VII, A, 229). He determined now to come out openly as a Christian author. In a very real sense he had always been that, as he insists. But hitherto he had communicated his teaching indirectly, under cover of pseudonymity. From this time he eschewed pseudonymity, at any rate in the main, and wrote specifically Christian works in his own name. He had learnt from the *Corsair* attacks what 'Christian collision' meant, and he knew on which side he stood. Three 'Edifying Discourses in Different Vein' (i.e. from the previous ones), published on 13 March 1847, began a series of Christian writings. 'From now on, there must be a forward movement into Christianity', he wrote in August or September 1847 (*Papirer*, VIII, A, 229). Now he 'wills one thing' only—to present Christianity open and neat. He never flinched again from this task.

In 1846 he had become interested in the case of a Bornholm priest named Adler, who had been suspended from his job for claiming to have direct revelations from Christ. As a result of Kierkegaard's cogitations, we have his profound treatise *On Authority and Revelation.* Also two *Minor Ethico-Religious Treatises* dealing with particular aspects of the main theme.

In 1848 Kierkegaard went through yet a further decisive religious experience, which only deepened his resolve to 'will one thing'. On Wednesday, 19 April, that year, he wrote, 'My whole being is changed. My reserve and self-isolation is broken. I must speak' (*Journals*,

747=*Papirer*, VII, A, 641). He realized that all his qualms about his own weaknesses and inhibitions—especially the one he calls his 'thorn in the flesh', must be and could be overcome. He consulted a doctor to see if this 'misrelationship between soul and body' could be cured medically, but was of course told that this was impossible. But, he writes, 'I shall now, with God's help, become myself. I believe in the fact that Christ will help me to conquer my introspective broodiness' (*Journals*, 748=*Papirer*, VII, A, 641). That faith was fully justified. Kierkegaard did conquer.

Strong and determined as he now was, he came more and more to feel that the Christianity presented by the Danish Church was weak and emaciated; and he was led, towards the close of his life, to attack that Church bitterly. Part III of the present work deals more fully with this attack and its effects. It is undoubtedly all too full of violence and bitterness, and is undoubtedly overdriven. But it cannot be by-passed as of no value. It is too full of home truths for that. What it does not involve is any attack on the concept Church as such. You may attack a Church, indeed every existing Church, without attacking *the* Church, in the widest sense of that term.

Because of the attack, a commotion was expected at Kierkegaard's funeral. What actually happened, both at the funeral service in church and at the graveside afterwards, will appear more fully in the following pages.

Kierkegaard died in Frederiks Hospital, Copenhagen, on 11 November 1855. His medical report there says, 'About 14 days ago, as he sat on a settee, he slid to the ground while leaning forward from it, and only got up with difficulty. He could still talk for a time after this, but next day when dressing he fell again. There was no swooning or convulsion or loss of consciousness; only a feeling of impotence. He could not lift himself upright; for some time his legs would not support him, but he did get up again eventually.'[1] The date of this medical report is 2 October 1855, the day when he collapsed in the street, and was taken straight to hospital. While there, he was lovingly cared for by his nephews Henrik and Michael Lund, house-surgeons, and by the Matron, Miss Ilia Fibiger.[2]

[1] *Breve og Aktstykke*, p. 21.
[2] See p. 101 ff below, and Geismar, VI, p. 97.

HANS BRØCHNER

Part I

HANS BRØCHNER

INTRODUCTORY NOTE

We are fortunate in possessing these *Recollections* from one of Kierkegaard's intimate friends who was also a very distant relation. In the last nineteen years of Kierkegaard's life, i.e. from 1836 to 1855, the two men knew each other well. Born in Fredericia, Brøchner (1820–75) became a philosopher of the type who take the 'myth' of Christianity to be of no account, and reduce religion to a kind of mystic inner feeling with no objective or historical basis. He went up to Copenhagen University in 1836, and lived with an uncle, Michael Andersen Kierkegaard, referred to in these pages) in Købmagergade.[1] In 1841 Brøchner was refused permission to take the theological examination because of his unorthodox views. His general attitude is indicated by the fact that he translated Strauss's *Die Christliche Glaubenslehre*, and was supported by Feuerbach when he attacked Martensen's more orthodox views on Baptism.[2] Brøchner travelled to Rome as a young man and there met Constanza Testa, to whom, in 1852, he became engaged. She, however, was a Roman Catholic and he a free-thinker, and her parents refused the marriage. Brøchner was deeply influenced by this experience, and the two carried on a correspondence all their lives. In 1854 Brøchner entered parliament as a member for Fredericia. He had worked as a private teacher or 'Docent' in Copenhagen University from 1849, and as an 'Extraordinary Docent' from 1857. To qualify for the latter post, he wrote a dissertation on Spinoza. In 1868 he wrote *The Problem of Faith and Knowledge*,[3] his first open attack on the 'Dualism' of Martensen, Kierkegaard, and Martin Nielsen. In 1862 he married Ingeborg Dorothea Ipsen, but after only four years she died (in 1866). In his last years Brøchner suffered from a chest disease.

Søren Kierkegaard and Brøchner were slightly related, since Brøchner's aunt (his mother's sister) was married to Michael Andersen Kierkegaard (1687–1776) (cf. extract 1 and *passim*). Søren Kierkegaard's grandfather was this Michael Andersen's brother—thus Søren Kierkegaard and Brøchner were distant cousins.

Now Kierkegaard was an orthodox Christian, and Brøchner was a free thinker. Their viewpoints differed, but it is to the credit of both that their friendship was not impaired. Undoubtedly

[1] The syllables *-gade* in this and similar words means 'street'. I have always retained *gade* when streets are mentioned, because it looks so odd otherwise. Similarly *-torv* (as, e.g. in Gammeltorv often mentioned) means 'market'.

[2] See extract 16.

[3] See extract 17.

Brøchner talked with his friends and pupils (among who was Georg Brandes) about Kierkegaard. For in his biography of Søren Kierkegaard (p. 10, 1877) Brandes tells of those peculiar 'walks' (or was it only one?) which Kierkegaard had with his father round the room, when, imagining they were out of doors, they described so vividly what they saw in imagination. True the account of these 'walks' had already been published by Barfod in 1872, in Vol. II of Kierkegaard's *Efterladte Papirer*, p. 78 ff. But Brandes says, 'The features of these walks were known to me before the *Papirer* came out, for Kierkegaard had told them to the late Professor Brøchner as being actual experiences of his own childhood.' (Brøchner does not mention these 'walks' in the present memoirs.)

Two further scraps of evidence that Brøchner talked with friends about Kierkegaard may be adduced, the first positive, the second conjectural:

(1) In Vol. I, p. 373, of *Letters to and from Northern Authors and Scientists*, by Georg and Edward Brandes, Georg says that he can dimly remember Brøchner telling him of the sin which Søren Kierkegaard thought he had discovered in his (Kierkegaard's) father's life, when he (Søren) was twenty-five years old. (Brøchner does not mention this either, in the present memoirs.)

(2) H. P. Barfod, editor of the first edition of Kierkegaard's *Papirer*, says (see *Efterladte Papirer*, I, p. lv), 'Søren Kierkegaard frequently entered into friendly conversation with a theologian known to incline towards atheism.' The context suggests this 'atheistic theologian' was Brøchner.

Brøchner then was in close contact with Kierkegaard, and still remembered him vividly, long after his death. Brøchner died in 1875, and left all his papers and manuscripts to C. K. F. Molbech. Among them were the present *Recollections*. These were first published in 1877 in a magazine edited by Georg and Edward Brandes, entitled *The Nineteenth Century* (Vol. V, p. 337–74).[1] They were published under the signature of Harold Høffding, but from what has been said above, we may readily assume that Georg Brandes would be behind the publication. Indeed in Brøchner's manuscripts there are many corrections and changes in G. Brandes' handwriting, and these are retained in *The Nineteenth Century*. Perhaps Høffding was chosen to 'publish' the *Recollections* because he, a philosophic author, followed in Brøchner's footsteps. The *Recollections* have often been cited by authors writing on Kierkegaard; but they have

[1] They have been re-published by Gyldendal (1953) in an attractive edition, with notes by Steen Johansen. I express my gratitude to this edition and its editor for many helpful suggestions. (T. H. C.).

never before been published in English except a minute fragment, in Dru's translation of Kierkegaard's *Journals*, p. 563. In *The Nineteenth Century*, small cuts were made, in deference to persons then living. In the present translation, these cuts are disregarded and Brøchner's original text is given in full.

Brøchner tells us that he wrote down these recollections between 12 December 1871 and 10 January 1872, i.e. during the Christmas holidays. Why just then? Because Kierkegaard's name had recently been before him in two different contexts:

(1) Vol. I of Martensen's *Christian Ethics* (which Brøchner would certainly have read) had recently appeared, and in it Kierkegaard is sharply criticized.

(2) Brøchner had lately received a letter from Pastor Barfod about Kierkegaard.

The letter from Barfod[1] asks if Brøchner could clarify an entry by Kierkegaard, written (in 1847?) on a loose slip of paper. The entry reads, 'I see from the papers that my full name has appeared on the placards, and that "I" am a character on the stage, and that the actor who played "me" performed so skilfully that he was greeted with acclamation.'[2] Brøchner replied in November 1871 to Barfod saying that Kierkegaard was mistaken. A student play by Pastor Hostrup called *The People Opposite* was produced in 1844, and Brøchner, then a student, played a character called Søren Kirk, caricaturing a certain civil servant named Ole Kirk. Hostrup had come to realize the possible confusion with Søren Kierkegaard, and had changed the character's name to Søren Trop; and so it remains. It seems that the *Norwegian Times*, reviewing the play (which was still being played three years later and is often played today), had spoken of 'Kierkegaardian syllogisms' in the play[3] and this was quoted in the *Copenhagen Flying Post*, 6 December 1847. Hence Kierkegaard's agitation.[4]

Brøchner's *Recollections* are written in a magnanimous spirit. He often lets Kierkegaard himself speak, but he delicately refrains from mentioning Kierkegaard's more intimate experiences—his engagement to Regine Olsen for example, about which he must have known. But as Georg Brandes says (*Collected Works*, II, p. 436), 'The picture the book gives us is, with all its unpretentiousness, sharply outlined. Every word sounds as if it came from actual life. Even the most insignificant details are alive.'

A more systematic view of Kierkegaard as an author is given us

[1] Barfod was engaged in producing a selection from the *Efterladte Papirer* (*E.P.*).
[2] *E.P.*, II, p. 328 f., and *Papirer*, VIII, A, 654.
[3] The play does rather take off the grandiose arguing of the times.
[4] See entry 23.

in Brøchner's *Problem of Faith and Knowledge*, pp. 118 ff. An excellent summary too is given in Brøchner's notice about Kierkegaard in *The Fatherland*, 1 December 1855.

A volume of letters from Brøchner to K. K. Molbeck has been published by Harold Hoffding (1902). From this volume I give two extracts.

THE RECOLLECTIONS

Recollections of Søren Kierkegaard, by H. Brøchner, written between 27 December 1871 and 10 January 1872.

I have tried to put down some recollections I have of Søren Kierkegaard. They cover a period of many years, and I think they may be of interest. Some day perhaps, when Søren Kierkegaard finds a competent biographer, they may contribute towards making his picture in certain respects more complete and more vivid. I note down my reminiscences merely as material for such a picture of Søren Kierkegaard, and have therefore not troubled to mould them into a whole, or give them shape by collecting them into well defined sections. I give them just as I retain them in my mind. They are my first impressions of particular incidents; and my memory is reliable.

1

My first meeting with Søren Kierkegaard was immediately after becoming a 'student'[1] (1836). I saw him then at the home of my old shopkeeper 'uncle',[2] M. A. Kierkegaard. It was at a party held on the occasion of the present Bishop Kierkegaard's engagement (or wedding?).[3] I saw Søren Kierkegaard without knowing who he was[4]; I was only told that he was Dr. Kierkegaard's brother. He spoke very little that evening, but obviously was observing everything closely. The only definite impression I then got was of his outward appearance, and that rather amused me. He was at that time twenty-three years old, and there was something very unruly in his whole appearance. He had a remarkable coiffure[5]; his hair was brushed up into a tufted cock's comb almost six inches above his forehead, and he looked very dishevelled in consequence. I formed the impression, without quite knowing why, that he was a shop assistant —perhaps because the family were tradespeople—and I immediately

[1] i.e. Passing the matriculation examination for admission to the University.

[2] Really his aunt's husband, who was a silk and hosiery salesman, living at 45 Købmagergade. He was Kierkegaard's father's second cousin; and so Søren Kierkegaard and Brøchner were second cousins. Brøchner lived with this uncle for quite ten years 1836–46. He had come up to the University from Fredericia.

[3] It must have been the wedding of Dr. P. Kierkegaard, 21 Oct. 1836, for Brøchner came up to the University from Fredericia in Oct. 1836, aged sixteen years.

[4] Brøchner was fresh from the provinces and did not know that Kierkegaard was already known in academic circles, through newspaper articles, his speeches in the Students' Union, etc.

[5] See illustration I.

jumped to the conclusion from his odd appearance that he must be a draper's assistant. I have often laughed heartily at my sharpness of perception!

2

After this party, Søren Kierkegaard and I met from time to time at my 'uncle's' home. By this time I had become on more intimate terms with him, and I soon noticed that his place was certainly not behind a counter, with a two-foot measure in his hand. He enjoyed propounding small paradoxes to the very ordinary circles there. I remember for example that he once surprised his relations by declaring, with the most serious face in the world, that he found the A.B.C. we used in our childhood to be one of the most interesting books in existence. He said he still read it very frequently, and got much profit from it.[1]

One evening he played Boston[2] with us. It was played with three variations, one of which consisted in three of the players being given seventeen cards each, and the fourth only one. The three others then gave away four cards each to this fourth person. Card games were played with almost devout seriousness in this house, and the fourth person's position in the game was always regarded as extremely doleful. But Søren Kierkegaard again surprised us greatly by asserting that the fourth player's position was quite the best imaginable, and that he wished always to be the fourth man.

3

In 1837 I sometimes used to meet Kierkegaard in a restaurant. At that time he no longer lived with his father, but in a house in Løvstræde, the house where Reitzel's bookshop now (1871) is.[3] He usually took his evening meal in a restaurant, and I can remember being surprised at the luxuriousness Søren Kierkegaard displayed by eating in the evening, with half a bottle of wine and such like, while I myself occasionally had a 'half beef'. We conversed fairly frequently, and he showed much friendliness towards me. One evening he asked me what aesthetic works I had read. I took the opportunity

[1] Sejer Kühle, *S. K. Barndom & Ungdom*, pp. 100–101, quotes one of Kierkegaard's fellow students, J. A. Østerman, as saying, 'His vivid intellect seized upon everything as a field for his brilliant dialectic and wit, no matter whether the thing was true or not.' And Kühle adds, 'It is undoubtedly true that K. let loose his witty dialectic upon everything; but no one noticed that something else besides the mere play and richness of intellect interested him.'

[2] = whist. So called after the seige of Boston (during the American Wars of Independence) to which the name reverts.

[3] It was about 1 Scpt. 1837, that K. moved to this address. For a list of K.'s dwellings, see Brandt and Ramel, *Kierkegaard & Pengene*, p. 130. This particular address is only known from this mention of Brøchner.

MICHAEL KIERKEGAARD
Father of Søren Kierkegaard

to hint, that I had not much access to them, and that I was very ignorant in many spheres. He asked me if I knew the German romantic writings, and I had to say I did not. He then asked me to walk home with him, and lent me a book of Eichendorff, *Dichter und ihre Gesellen.*[1] (I have since bought the very copy at the auction of his books after his death. It serves as a memorial of this meeting with him.) I remember taking it back to him after about a fortnight, excusing myself for keeping it so long. (I was zealously studying theology at that time.) To my surprise he countered by asking me if I had finished reading it *already*. He obviously could see with his sharp glance, that 'No' hovered on my tongue, and he enjoyed embarrassing me, in so goodly a fashion—which on this occasion was all too easy. I blushed a little, and that sight always attracted him in the 'young man'.[2]

Two things stand out in my memory from this visit to his home when he lent me that book. One is my astonishment at his large library, which considerably impressed me.[3] The other was a thing peculiar to Søren Kierkegaard. He was going out again after lending me the book, and as we were going away he blew out a candle he had lit. He explained that he always did this with some care and at some distance, because he had persuaded himself into believing that the smoke of a candle was dangerous to inhale, and might injure his chest.

4

In 1838 Søren Kierkegaard's father died. I had only seen his father once, at my old uncle Kierkegaard's house, mentioned above. The father was a remarkable character, whose appearance impressed itself vividly on my memory. He walked with my uncle up and down the floor of my uncle's dining-room, conversing with him. He was somewhat bent in his gait; his carriage corresponded to the thoughtful and serious expression of his face; and his grey hair was smoothed back behind his ears, which made his face the more sharply outlined. The respect and love which Søren Kierkegaard felt for his father finds vivid expression in his works.[4] The old man was a most conscientious person, most scrupulous in money matters, frugal in daily life,

[1] This novel came out in 1834. K. quotes from it in *Papirer* II, A, 404. K. was much interested in German Romanticists—Eichendorff, Arnim, Hoffmann, Chamisso. There is a quotation from Eichendorff's *Digest vor der Stadt* in *Either/Or*, I, p. 295 (I, p. 377), a quotation from *Krieg den Philisten* (1824) in I, A, 157, and an analysis of *Viel Lärmen um Nichts* (1833) in I, C, 86, and a passing reference in *The Concept of Irony* (XIII, p. 382) to Eichendorff's *Aus dem Leben eines Taugenichts.*

[2] Brøchner here suggests that he has served as a model for the 'young man' in the *Stages on Life's Way.*

[3] At his death Kierkegaard had 2,748 books. They were sold by auction in 1836, and Brøchner was one of the buyers. See Kühle, *Berlingske Aftenavis*, 24 Feb. 1943.

[4] See, e.g., the fact that so many of Kierkegaard's works are dedicated to his father.

but open-handed on special occasions. Søren Kierkegaard once told me how, when he had taken a journey to North Sjælland,[1] his old father had provided him generously with money, and still more, had surprised him by sending him, at one of the last coach stations, a money-order for 50 Rigs-dollars. Søren Kierkegaard once said, when talking to Magister Adler,[2] about his father's conscientiousness, 'My father was born on quarter-day.'

When Søren left his father's house, the old man gave him a yearly sum which by the standards of that time was very liberal; if I am not mistaken it was 800 dollars (Rigsdaler) per year. [According to S.K. himself, 500. See Ammundsen, *S.K.'s Youth*, p. 123].

5

My sister Hansine, now passed away,[3] was in Copenhagen in 1839, as a young girl. Once when I happened to mention Søren Kierkegaard's name, she told me that she had seen him once, before her confirmation, when she was visiting our old uncle, M. A. Kierkegaard. Our cousins[4] had one day advised her, when Søren Kierkegaard was expected, not to engage in conversation with him, because he was 'a dreadfully spoilt and naughty boy, who always hung about his mother's skirts'. My sister was then about thirteen years old, and Søren fifteen. Later in life she read some of his devotional treatises with great joy, notably *The Works of Love*; and she would remind me sometimes, with a characteristic smile of hers, of the warning our cousins had then given her.

6

Shortly after Kierkegaard had taken his theological degree,[5] he told me in conversation that his father had always wished him to take the theological examination, and that they had very frequently discussed the matter. 'So long as father lived, however, I was able to defend my thesis that I ought not to take it. But when he was dead, I had to take over his part in the debate as well as my own, and then I could no longer hold out, but had to decide to read for the examination.' He did so, with great energy. He took 'his Brøchner' as tutor,[6] worked through the most barren subjects, made excerpts of Church History, learnt the list of names of the Popes by heart—and so on. His tutor was very pleased with him.

[1] To Gilleleje in 1835. [2] See note to No. 20, below. [3] She died in 1869.

[4] I.e. the three daughters of M. A. Kierkegaard, two of whom still lived with their father at the time Brøchner is speaking of, 1828.

[5] Kierkegaard got first-class honours, 3 July 1840.

[6] Not our Brøchner, but one Hans Brøchner, cousin to our author's father. Kierkegaard used to use the adjective 'my' of all who served him, my shoemaker, my fruiterer, my driver, etc. He was upbraided for this once by Regine Olsen's brother. In one letter to her Kierkegaard mentions this (R. Meyer, *Forlovesen*, p. 8).

Shortly after Kierkegaard had passed his examination Peter Stilling (later D.Phil.)[1] went to 'his' (i.e. the same) Brøchner for tuition also, saying he thought he might be ready 'in a year and a half: Kierkegaard I think did not take longer'. 'Right,' said old Brøchner, who exuded courtesy, 'but don't imagine *you* can do that. With Kierkegaard it was different, he could do anything.'

I remember that in 1839 Søren Kierkegaard and I started attending a special course with written theological exercises, held by Clausen.[2] Kierkegaard, however, only attended the first two or three classes. It is said that many years earlier he had attended a similar course by Clausen, and once, instead of answering the question set, he had analysed it and shown that the question itself was meaningless. Unfortunately Clausen was offended, and Kierkegaard ceased to attend the course.

In the written theological examination, Kierkegaard came fourth.[3] Before him came M. Wad, Warburg, and Chr. F. Christens. The examiners declared, however, that Kierkegaard's essays showed far greater maturity and development of thought than some of the others. But the essays of these three, they said, contained a richer measure of positive theological material.

7

In the same conversation in which Kierkegaard told me how he had come to take his theological examination, he also spoke of his father's wonderfully calm objectivity. For instance, the old man once said to Søren, 'It would be a good thing for you if I were dead. Then you might still perhaps become something. But as long as I live you will not.'[4]

Another characteristic of his father was once told me by my departed cousin Peter Kierkegaard.[5] When Søren Kierkegaard's mother died,[6] his father was deeply distressed. At the funeral Bishop Mynster called on him and, much moved, expressed his sympathy. The old man, without revealing his own sorrow, listened to Mynster whom he valued highly, and when Mynster had finished he

[1] 1812–69, philosophic writer.

[2] In the winter term of 1839–40 Clausen held such a course every Friday, 9–11 a.m. Martensen, who also attended, said they were 'mighty learned'! (*Levnet*, I, p. 56.)

[3] In Kierkegaard's examination there were sixty-three candidates. Twenty-seven got a first (*laudabilis*), of whom Kierkegaard was the fourth best. Wad ended as priest at Korsør, Warburg at Asminderød, Christens became a schoolmaster and author of pedagogic works.

[4] Cf. *Journals*, 747 (VIII, A, 640): 'You will never do any good so long as you have money.'

[5] Son of the above-mentioned tradesman, M. A. Kierkegaard. He was a cripple. See No. 43 below.

[6] She died 30 July 1834, and was buried 4 Aug. in the Assistance Kierkegaard.

said, 'Shall we, your grace, go into the study and drink a glass of wine?' Mynster, who knew the old man, did not misunderstand what this meant.

8

While Søren Kierkegaard was in Berlin in the winter of 1841–2,[1] I presented myself as candidate for a theological degree, but because of my unorthodox views I was rejected. I corresponded with Chr. F. Christens[2] who was also in Berlin, and who sent greetings from Kierkegaard which I returned through Christens.

Shortly after Kierkegaard's return I met him in the street. He was very friendly, spoke of my doings and studies, and told me that while in Berlin he had longed for many things at home, among which was to see me. He could say such things with a characteristically winning expression. His smile and his look were expressive to a degree difficult to describe. He had a way of greeting one at a distance with a look. It was only a little movement of the eye, and yet the expression meant so much. There was at times something infinitely gentle and loving in his look, but also something goading and irritating. He was able with a glance to 'put himself *en rapport*' with a passer-by, as he expressed it. Anybody meeting that glance was either attracted or else repelled, made embarrassed, uncertain, or irritated.

I once walked through a whole street with him while he explained how one can make psychological studies by so putting oneself *en rapport* to passers-by.[3] As he explained his theory he put it in practice with almost everybody we met. There was no one on whom his glance did not make an obvious impression. On the same occasion he surprised me by the easy way he took up a conversation with all sorts of people. In some few talks he picked up an earlier conversation and carried it forward to a point where he could pick it up again as opportunity served.

The occasion of these experiments was this. I was walking before him deep in thought, and had not heard him call me, nor noticed that he tapped me on the shoulder. When finally I did notice, he said that it was wrong to be so immersed in oneself, and not make the

[1] Kierkegaard left Copenhagen for Berlin on 25 Oct. 1841, fourteen days after the final breach with his fiancée, Regine Olsen, on 11 Oct. 1841. While there he attended Schelling's lectures. He was back in Copenhagen on 6 March 1842.

[2] See p. 11 note 3.

[3] The actress Julie Sørdring says that her father loved to walk out with Søren Kierkegaard because both 'loved experimenting'. They once, e.g., gave a poor woman a note for five Rigsdaler (a large sum) just to enjoy her surprise. Kierkegaard used to 'hump along with his short trouser legs, swinging his little cane' (*Memoirs*, I, p. 183). Cf. Arthur Abrahams, *Minder*, 1895, p. 55, where he speaks of S.K.'s 'uneasy and somewhat skipping gait'.

observations one might in so rich a field. To show me his method he dragged me up and down several streets, and surprised me by his talent for psychological experiment. He was always interesting to accompany, but there was one drawback. His movements were so irregular because of his crooked figure that you could never walk straight when he was with you. You were successively pushed in towards the houses and cellar-holes, and out towards the gutter. And when he gesticulated with his arm and his Spanish cane, walking became still more difficult. You had from time to time to get round the other side of him to keep your place!

9

The winter Søren Kierkegaard spent in Berlin, he consorted with Danes, of whom not a few had come to hear Schelling. Among them was my friend Christian Fenger Christens. Søren Kierkegaard spoke of Christens with great appreciation. He told me later that Christens was the cleverest of all the Danes who had been in Berlin that winter; and among them were such men as A. F. Krieger, then jurist, now minister, and Carl Weis, then military adviser, now head of a department in the Cultus-Ministry. Christens told me various little things about Kierkegaard; about his helplessness in speaking German, notably when he had to speak of things in daily life (for example, on his first evening in Berlin, he did not know how to say he wanted a candlestick); about how his host swindled him, and as his swindlings increased elevated him from Magister to Doctor and then to Professor (this amused Kierkegaard himself when he discovered the reason); about his embarrassment when Weis, who appreciated an elegant dinner, one day took him to a first-class restaurant where a number of elegantly clad gentlemen in black coats with white cravats and ties, were standing in the corners of the room. After Kierkegaard had greeted them respectfully, he and Weis sat down at a table; whereupon the said gentlemen sprang forward; and showed themselves to be the waiters!

Christens told me also how Kierkegaard enjoyed himself in Berlin by getting Licentiate (now Dean) Rothe into difficulties. Rothe had been abroad for some time and had attended lectures in Strasbourg and elsewhere. He was very selfconscious about all the learning he had accumulated. Kierkegaard nearly always, when they met, got him to talk about the really essential outcome of his travels from the speculative-philosophy point of view. When Rothe said anything that won approval, Kierkegaard always knew how to show him either that this was something very old, or to ask little questions about 'something which he did not quite understand' in what was said. This brought the poor man into such confusion (for he was not a very deep thinker) that he hardly knew where he was. When Kierkegaard had brought him to this point, he would suddenly remember that he was very busy and had an engagement somewhere and had to go. He left the poor licentiate in the midst of his confusion, to the amusement of the others.

In *Either/Or* Kierkegaard has described this very method he employed on a licentiate. I wonder if he had his Berlin acquaintance in mind when he wrote those pages.[1]

10

Not long after Kierkegaard returned home, he spoke to me about his studies. I told him what Greek authors I had read to date, and touched on the waxing interest I was getting for Greek poetry and philosophy. He encouraged me to continue these studies, and spoke warmly of the significance of Greek culture for our age.[2] He used this expression, 'Greece ought always to have a representative in our age, just as one Power has a representative among other Powers to look after its interests.' Kierkegaard himself had a good knowledge of Greek, and had read not a little. His works bear witness how well he had grasped the Greek spirit.

11

In 1842 a little pseudonymous work was published, *Johan Ludvig Heiberg after Death.*[3] I knew about this before it was published, and spoke of it to Søren Kierkegaard. He was not pleased that Heiberg was made the object of such mockery, and spoke with much warmth of his importance as an aesthete in our country, and especially as the foremost teacher, in his day, of aesthetics in Denmark. Kierkegaard put Heiberg over all the contemporary aesthetic writers in Germany. (Only minor works of Vischer[4] had been published.) Later on, after *Either/Or* was published and Heiberg had written his well-known review of it,[5] Kierkegaard once spoke to me about Heiberg and revealed his displeasure at this effusion. He recognized

[1] *Either/Or*, I, p. 246 (I, p. 313), but no licentiate is specifically mentioned.

[2] Rejected as he was by the Theological Faculty of the University, Brøchner took up Oriental languages, and in 1845 took his M.A. in Semitic languages, Latin, Greek, and the Philosophy of History.

[3] *J. L. Heiberg after Death, Apocalyptic Comedy in 5 Acts*, by Adam Howitz. The real author was C. K. F. Molbech (see introduction), with Brøchner himself as assistant! It is a parody of Heiberg's *A Soul After Death.*

[4] Friedrich Theodor Vischer (1807–87). His chief works appeared 1846–57.

[5] *Either/Or* appeared 20 Feb. 1843, and Heiberg's review in *Intelligensblade* 1 March 1843. For Kierkegaard's opinions on this review see *Journals*, 464 (IV, A, 162). See also IV, B, 26–58. Here he says Heiberg has changed in the last thirteen to fifteen years. The same accusation is repeated in *Samlede Værker*, V, p. 28.

Heiberg's importance as an aesthete, but stressed his limitations. 'I should like to bring forward a whole lot of aesthetic problems of which Heiberg has no suspicion.' No doubt Kierkegaard was thinking of the problems which have now been dealt with in the *Stages* and *Postscript*.

12

During these years I met Kierkegaard frequently when I went out for walks in the evening. I usually made for Frederiksberg Gardens. Kierkegaard went there too, but stopped at the garden gate where small flower borders flank the (at the time) narrow paths leading from the gate to the first open place. He would inhale the scent of the flowers for a few moments, and then take away the memory of this 'moment' with him. That was the way he liked to terminate and limit his walks. His walks had a definite aim,[1] but this aim was so to say only touched upon. There was no dwelling upon it. Only such a preamble of enjoyment was taken as could be ideally worked out later.

I remember an amusing incident on one of these evening walks. When we were returning from the garden to the allé we had to pass the posts at the end of the footpath between the trees. We found that the posts had been newly painted. Kierkegaard not noticing this, put his hand on one of them as we passed between. He soon realized that his hand was all over paint, and so, while still talking, he made several unsuccessful attempts (with the inevitable cane under his arm) to wash the paint off by rubbing the moist, dewy, overhanging leaves of trees between his hands. His efforts brought many a smile on the faces of the passers-by.

13

About this time I sometimes saw Søren Kierkegaard on horseback.[2] He had learnt to ride for the sake of the exercise, and also to be able to take small excursions independently of a coach-driver. He did not cut a particularly good figure on horseback. One saw from his posture that he did not trust his ability to control the horse if it should decide to become fractious. He sat upright, and gave one the impression that he was all the time trying to follow his riding-master's instructions. He could scarcely, when he was on horseback, have had much freedom for rumination and imagination.

[1] Cf. entry 26, where Brøchner speaks of Søren Kierkegaard in Berlin, 1846.

[2] We know that Kierkegaard learnt to ride in 1840. Meyer (*Forlovelsen*, p. 23), gives a letter from Kierkegaard to Regine which says, 'Now it is winter, but therefore just the time to think of summer. My horse snorts, the reins are loose in my hands, Nature wakens . . .' and he describes a ride in the country.

Indeed he soon gave up horse-riding, and preferred a carriage when he wanted to visit his favourite spots in the woods around Copenhagen. In the years when he was working hardest at his literary writings, these tours were one of the means he used to keep himself fresh, and to get himself into the right mood for his productions.

14

Let me here mention a remark he made somewhere about this time which is characteristic of the man. He had a servant[1] who was very trustworthy, and to whom he entrusted the carrying out of all sorts of practical matters. When he moved house, for example, he would drive off in the morning and come back in the evening to his new abode, there to find everything in complete order, even to the perfect arrangement of his books. This was all the work of this servant Anders. Kierkegaard once said, speaking of Anders' practical talent, 'He is in truth *my body*.'

15

When *Either/Or* was first published, I had many talks with him about the book. I had immediately recognized that the anonymous author was Kierkegaard through reading the *Diapsalmata*.[2] For I came across words which he had already let slip to me in our conversations. I never of course tried to make Kierkegaard confess himself the author. But where I found anything obscure, I spoke to him about it as to an elder person who had richer insight. In this way I got many quite close expositions of the book's themes, and he spoke to me about the work with a freedom he would hardly have shown if I had been indiscreet. One point on which he often dwelt was the polemic element in Pt. I. He told me one day with great vivacity how in many places there was a suitable *motif* for a poem (such *motifs*, however, were certainly not worked out in the continuing part of the book). For example, he mentioned the description of women's beauty and said that in each of these sentences, 'the little hand, the neat foot', etc. there was a *motif* for a sonnet.

He sometimes indicated the lines along which the problems handled in *Either/Or* could be carried forward; but I confess that I only understood many of his suggestions when his later writings came out.

[1] Anders Westergaard, see *Journals*, 752, 834, 1107 (VIII, A, 648; IX, A, 375; X³, A, 144). Many anecdotes are told of him, e.g. how he once asked Kierkegaard if he could give him proof of immortality. Kierkegaard replied that we are all ignorant on that subject. (Letter dated 12 Sept. 1869 from F. Schedte to Pastor Barfod, first editor of the *Papirer*.)

[2] See *Either/Or*, I, first section.

He liked to hear appreciative statements about the book. I said one day that no book had so set me thinking as *Either/Or*; not anyway since I first read Hegel's *Logic*. This obviously pleased him. We were just by the door of his house in Nørregade,[1] and were going our ways. He gave me a friendly hand as we parted; and with it the smile which I knew so well.

16

When I had published my book against Martensen[2] Kierkegaard discussed it with me. He was dissatisfied with a review in the *Berlingske Avis*. The review had adopted a superior tone, and with an air of authority had tried to squash the poor author. I told Kierkegaard that I had merely been amused at the review, since its forced Christianity looked a bit ludicrous when one remembered that the anonymous article appeared in a paper which was edited by a Jew!

Kierkegaard pointed out a certain statement in my little book that he wished had been omitted. It was where (with some derision of Martensen's attempt to assert the new-born babe's freedom) I said that the only free act you could speak of at a baptism was the baby's yelling when it is soused with water. This, thought Kierkegaard, sounded flippant and could easily be used malevolently by the ill-disposed.

17

Kierkegaard often spoke of Ludvig Feuerbach[3] when we were talking together. From oral statements made by Kierkegaard, I have stated in my *Problem of Faith and Knowledge* (1868) that there can be no doubt it is Feuerbach that Kierkegaard is aiming at in a quotation there adduced. He recognized the clarity and keenness with which Feuerbach had understood Christianity; but he asserted once in a conversation that from Feuerbach's enthusiasm for Nature (especially from the passion with which, in *Wesen des Christenthums*, he speaks of the strengthening power of water, both materially and spiritually)[4] he (Kierkegaard) had got the impression not only of a

[1] Kierkegaard lived from 1840 to 1844 in Nørregade 38.

[2] *Some Remarks about Baptism*, 26 June 1843. An answer to Martensen's *Christian Baptism*. Reviewed in the *Berlingske Tidende*, 29 June.

[3] Ludvig Feuerbach (1804–72), well-known German philosopher, whose best-known work, *Das Wesen des Christenthums*, came out in 1841. We have reference to this book in *Stages*, p. 415 (VI, p. 483), where Feuerbach is quoted as saying, 'Religious existence, and especially the Christian, is a constant history of suffering.' In *Stages*, p. 409 (VI, p. 475), Feuerbach is spoken of as knowing all about religion, and knowing, will have nothing to do with it. In the *Postscript*, p. 513 (VII, p. 570), Feuerbach is quoted as saying that all theology is anthropology. On p. 543 of the same book (VII, p. 605), it is Feuerbach that Kierkegaard is referring to when he speaks of 'a scoffer'.

[4] See *Wesen des Christenthums*, p. 321, where Feuerbach is saying that in baptism, ordinary natural water is invested with supernatural power. But 'the natural quality

strong sensuousness in Feuerbach, but also of discomfiture[1] through this sensuousness. Kierkegaard added, 'This is an opinion I should not of course express in print, but I can't get away from this impression. There is something in Feuerbach's characteristically passionate pathos, and in his antipathy to Christianity, which becomes clearer to me on this hypothesis.'

These words about Feuerbach led him to speak of characters in antiquity in whom a refined sensuousness appears. He drew for example a very imaginative picture of Maecenas, a man who 'certainly exhausted all the voluptuousness Rome could offer him'. He mentioned how Maecenas, when he could not sleep, sought to lull his senses by the splash of spring-water in his bedchamber, and by soft strains of distant music. Such scenes Kierkegaard could portray superbly. It was not, however, the poetic description, but psychological analysis or rather dissection, that interested him.

18

On a certain long walk somewhere about this time, I had occasion to observe how tellingly and forcefully Kierkegaard could declaim passages of poetry. He was speaking of Aladdin[2]; of the audacity and talent which characterizes his wishing; and he contrasted the brave daring of this talented hero, with the cautious calculations of the reflective mind. He then quoted Aladdin's words to the spirit, where he invites him to build that glorious palace for the wedding night. We had arrived outside Charlottenborg Castle. Kierkegaard stopped as he quoted these lines, which he accompanied with a little gesture of his arm. Colour came to his cheeks, and his glance became lit up and warm; his voice, though restrained, was like that of a prince who knows he has power to command.

19

On one occasion we talked about Hegel's exposition of the history of philosophy. Kierkegaard pronounced this to be at many points too subjective in conception. He said, 'Geniuses always lack

of the water has value and significance too, because the supernatural effects of baptism are conjoined to water only, not to any other substance'.

[1] Brøchner coins the word *Svækketedhed*, from *svække* which usually means to be defeated or discomfited in battle (see Exodus 17:13, in the Danish translation of 1931). I cannot see how sensuousness can be deduced from this passage alone in Feuerbach. He is indeed stating what seems to me to be true, the importance of the outer element in a sacrament (in the same context he mentions the bread and wine in Holy Communion, as well as water in baptism), because what it does in its natural, 'sensuous' state has a counterpart in the spiritual. Water cleanses; bread and wine feed. So, in the sacraments, they do spiritually. This is quite orthodox and innocent doctrine. But, in a wider sense, Feuerbach reproaches Christians for this very use of natural things, and for 'anthropomorphism'.

[2] Oehlenschlägers play of that name is meant. See Henriette's *Recollections*, p. 145.

the power of objectively grasping the thought of others. They always find their own.'

Not long afterwards, he made the remark, 'I have never had the faculty of understanding others objectively.' At that moment he had, I am sure, forgotten his earlier remark. But I remembered it, and I smiled to myself as I inwardly drew the obvious conclusion.

20

About the time when Magister Adler's[1] mental derangement began, Kierkegaard told me some curious things about him. Adler came to see Kierkegaard one day with a book he had published, and they had a long talk about their respective religious publications.[2] Adler gave Kierkegaard to understand that he regarded Kierkegaard as a kind of John the Baptist in relationship to himself. He (Adler) had received a direct revelation, and so was the real Messiah. I remember the smile with which Kierkegaard reported his own reply. He was quite satisfied, he had answered, with the position Adler had assigned to him, for he found it a most respectable job to be a John the Baptist, and had no ambition whatever to be a Messiah!

During the same visit Adler read a great part of his book to Kierkegaard, sometimes in his ordinary voice, sometimes in a funny sort of whisper. Kierkegaard ventured the remark that he found no new revelation in Adler's work; to which Adler replied, 'Then I will come again this evening and read the whole book to you with *this* voice (the whispering one). You will then see that my point will dawn upon you.'

In my early student years, about 1836–7, I once heard Adler speak of Kierkegaard. He remarked upon the intellectual quality of Kierkegaard's conversations, but thought that Kierkegaard sometimes prepared them beforehand.

21

As a young man (perhaps it was after 'defending'[3] his M.A. thesis), Kierkegaard considered the possibility of a job at the University. He soon, however, gave up the idea. He once told me that

[1] Adler published two books in 1843, and four in 1846, though these latter can hardly be meant at this point of time.

[2] A. P. Adler (1812–69) was a priest in Hasle on the Island of Bornholm who interested Kierkegaard greatly. See his great *Book about Adler*. Adler was suspended from his office in 1844 on the publication of *Some Sermons*, on the possible grounds of insanity; but certainly of heresy. He retired to Copenhagen in 1845, and this is probably the time referred to above. The *Book about Adler* is translated under the title *On Authority and Revelation.*

[3] This defending (or *Disputats* as it is called in Danish), is a public examination when the candidate had to 'defend' his thesis *viva voce.*

Sibbern[1] had bidden him seek a post as 'Docent'[2] (tutor) in philosophy. Kierkegaard replied that he would need a full year's preparation. 'Now how can you imagine that you will be given a job at your own convenience?' answered Sibbern. 'Well,' replied Kierkegaard, 'I could, I suppose, do like Rasmus Nielsen,[3] let myself be appointed without being prepared.' Sibbern became quite peevish and said, 'Must you always be making cuts at Nielsen?' Not long after Nielsen was appointed at the University.

Kierkegaard[4] spoke to me many times about Nielsen. Once, in Christian VIII's time, he mentioned that Nielsen had sought the King's protection, remarking sarcastically on Nielsen's canniness. ('He understands the Jutland saying that "a man must have something to live on",' said Kierkegaard.) Later on, however, when Nielsen and Kierkegaard were associates, Kierkegaard spoke of him with more interest, recognizing his ability. Kierkegaard once said to me, 'Nielsen is the only one of the younger talented authors risen up among us who will achieve anything.' It was, however, Nielsen's intellectual capacity, not his character, that Kierkegaard set store by.

When Kierkegaard was struggling with himself as to whether to attack the established church or not, we find him reflecting whether to initiate somebody into his thoughts (see the *Journals* of that date). He mentions Nielsen, who at that time was very closely associated with him, and whom he was then seeing every day. But Kierkegaard rejected the thought again with the hardly flattering remark, 'No, Nielsen is a self-advertiser.'[5]

22

In many of his writings, Kierkegaard has spoken about the attack of the *Corsair* upon him.[6] In these passages he looks at the

[1] F. C. Sibbern (1784–1872) was Professor of Philosophy from 1813 to 1870.

[2] The title of a supplementary teacher not a professor.

[3] Nielsen gave lectures as Privat-Docent in the winter terms of 1840–41, on Church History and New Testament exegesis. On 22 April 1841 he was elected Professor of Moral Philosophy, and the following summer lectured on Metaphysics.

[4] From here to the end of entry 21 was omitted from the first edition.

[5] The actual words do not seem to appear anywhere, but Nielsen is mentioned in the *Journals*, 862, 878, 905, 1032, 1182, 1194, 1220 (p. 442). See also Ch. XI of Hohlenberg's biography, *Kierkegaard*, which I have translated.

[6] The *Corsair*, a humorous journal sometimes claimed by the Danes to be the precursor of *Punch* (though it differed in being more closely personal), existed from 8 Oct. 1840 to 2 Oct. 1846. Its editor was M. A. Goldschmidt, a brilliant young Jew, much taken up with the new democratic ideas of the French Revolution. The paper used to caricature famous people, but, out of respect, Goldschmidt long refrained from attacking Kierkegaard. The latter, however, in the *Fatherland*, 27 Dec. 1845, asked to be attacked and Goldschmidt reluctantly agreed. Kierkegaard thought the paper a scandal, and this was his way of stopping the scandal. In fact the method succeeded in the end, because after one and a half years or so, the 'great look' that Kierkegaard once bestowed on Goldschmidt when he met him in the street, made Goldschmidt decide to give the paper up. He recognized Kierkegaard's superiority and innocence. But the attacks cost Kierkegaard endless ridicule. They went on for a year and a half,

matter from an ethical point of view, and undoubtedly assesses the value and meaning of the attack far too highly as regards the general public. Kierkegaard had not a sense of actuality, if I may use the expression, which, in a given situation, could form a balance to his enormous reflective powers. He could as it were reflect a bagatelle up to becoming of world-historic significance. This was undoubtedly so with the *Corsair*.

He once talked to me at great length about the *Corsair's* attitude, and condemned its wit-making. He did so from a purely aesthetic angle. His real grudge against the paper was that it destroyed any ideal sense of humour in the public, by fastening its gibes upon well-known people, who consequently were fixed once and for all in the reader's minds as comic characters. The reader laughed at what was said, not because it contained any worthy humour—but because, without being really comic, it was directed against people whom everybody from then onwards agreed *were* comic, and to be laughed at.

23

The same kind of thing which happened to Kierkegaard with the *Corsair's* attack happened to him also with 'Søren Kirk' in Hostrup's play, *The People Opposite*.[1] In his *Journals* Kierkegaard often says that Hostrup put him on the stage; and from the way he speaks, he clearly took this to heart. At the first performance I myself played the rôle of Søren Kirk, and I remember speaking to Kierkegaard about this at the time without feeling that he objected at all. But I suppose he reflected himself by degrees into another frame of mind. In this small part, Hostrup has admittedly taken *motifs* from Søren Kierkegaard's writings; but clearly his main idea in the part is to present the kind of dialectic which was prevalent in those years among the young students, especially after Martensen had given them an urge to affect a very superficial pursuit of philosophy. Kierkegaard was a master at this kind of dialectic in his youth—when he wanted to be!

My conversation with Kierkegaard about this rôle of Søren Kirk took place one evening when I was going to a rehearsal at the Hof-theatre. I met Kierkegaard in Højbro-plads. He stopped me and asked where I was going. I told him I was going to a rehearsal of Hostrup's play. 'Yes, you are going to play *me*,' said Kierkegaard. I replied that I was not going to play *him*, but the kind of dialectician we in Denmark were producing. We parted, and I had no suspicion that Kierkegaard took umbrage at me for having taken on the part.

mocking at Kierkegaard. We are more used to public caricatures, and there is not the same personal sting as in the limited circle of Copenhagen in Kierkegaard's day.

[1] See Introduction, p. 5 above.

In any case he surely must have been sufficiently aware of my general attitude towards him to know that it would never have occurred to me to mimic him or make fun of him. I had too much respect for him for that—and moreover I was much too bad an actor!

24

At the beginning of the '40's, Kierkegaard took a journey over to West Jutland to his father's birthplace.[1] He told me a characteristic little incident that happened while he was away. He was staying in his ancestral village,[2] where his father had left a large legacy to found a school.[3] Kierkegaard was received with great obsequiousness, and the schoolchildren were especially active. 'I was really afraid they would erect a triumphal arch for me,' he said. When he was about to depart he drove past the school. There stood the schoolmaster with all the children drawn up to sing a song, composed by the teacher in Søren Kierkegaard's honour. The teacher, who was to lead the singing, stood with a manuscript in his hand and was just going to give the sign to begin when Kierkegaard's carriage drew up beside him. Søren Kierkegaard bowed low to the schoolmaster with his most friendly smile, took the manuscript from his hands as if to read it through, and at the same time gave the driver a sign to drive on. That threw the whole formation of the children into confusion. The deacon[4] did not know his own poem by heart, and so could not get the song started because Kierkegaard had the manuscript. The children stood silent and confused, and Kierkegaard rolled off to the main road, nodding and bowing as he went; highly amused within himself at the schoolmaster's disappointment.[5]

25

On the day that J. F. Hagen, Lic. Theol. (later Professor of Theology), had 'disputed',[6] I discussed Hagen's thesis 'On Marriage' with Kierkegaard. I had publicly opposed the thesis. Kierkegaard was not satisfied with it: he found the whole treatment superficial and he adumbrated to me something of what is given in fuller form

[1] See *Kierkegaard's Journey to Jutland* by T. H. Croxall (Danish Tourist Association), translating the relevant sections of *Papirer*, III, 14–84. The journey took from about 19 July to 6 Aug. 1840.

[2] *Sæding*, near Ringkøbing.

[3] A tablet in Sæding church describes this.

[4] The village schoolmaster was and still often is, the 'deacon' of the church, whose duties are to keep the registers, lead the singing, and help generally in Divine Service.

[5] This is a disgraceful story, and can only be excused, if at all, as a young man's prank. Of course we do not know the schoolmaster!

[6] Johan Fredrik Hagen (1817–59) 'disputed' 14 July 1845 for his licentiate degree. His thesis was 'Marriage, viewed from an Ethical and Historical Point of View'. Hans Brøchner was one of the opponents *ex auditorio*.

by his pseudonyms.[1] He also mentioned on this same occasion the Germans' thorough treatment of such subjects, and said, with reference to Hagen's essay, 'We ought to take care to look a bit decent, if such books are to be read by the Germans.'

26

While I was staying in Berlin in the summer of 1846, Kierkegaard turned up.[2] It was one of the short sojourns abroad he sometimes took when he wanted to work really intensively. He would seek a change of surroundings in order to catch the right mood.[3] I met him quite unexpectedly in a restaurant where I used to eat, and where he went, I imagine, to meet his own countrymen; for during his first stay in Berlin this restaurant was the meeting place of all the Danes. He did not think much of it as a restaurant. It was restricted, he said, 'to the lowest conception of an order'. He came forward to meet me with friendliness, and invited me to dine with him next day at his hotel. He also took some long walks with me in the few days he was in Berlin. I was fairly thrilled with all the new things I came upon in Berlin, and was indefatigably active. Kierkegaard was amused at this activity. I even went so far as to attend the meetings of a Democratic Workers' Union. We talked together a good deal about things in Berlin, about things at home, about my D.Phil. thesis[4]—and so on. On our walks I noticed that Kierkegaard generally sought out certain particular spots which he was fond of. For instance, in the *Thiergarten* there was a lovely spot surrounded by flower-borders. He made this the goal of his walks, just as the flower-beds near the entrance to Fredriksberg Garden[5] had been his goal in Copenhagen. Perhaps he was reminded of the latter; and hence became attached to this place in the *Thiergarten*.

Once, when visiting him at his hotel, I noticed with what richness of imagination everything in his rooms was arranged so as to conduce to the right mood for his work: the lighting, the communication between the rooms, the arrangement of the furniture—everything was arranged to a definite plan. Kierkegaard was very meticulous about service, but very liberal with his tips. Our little dinner for two

[1] Hagen in his thesis, p. 150, refers to Victor Emerita's *Either/Or*, I. It is, however, in *Either/Or*, II, and in the *Stages* that the long essays by 'the married man' (*alias* B) come.

[2] This was the last of four journeys Kierkegaard made to Berlin. He left Copenhagen on 2 May 1846 by the steamer *Geiser*, and travelled *via* Stettin; returning by the same ship on 16 May.

[3] If Kierkegaard was at work on a book, it may have been the *Book on Adler*, which he was working at during the summer of 1846.

[4] Brøchner 'disputed' 1 Nov. 1846 for the 'Master of Philosophy' as it then was, with a thesis entitled, 'The Position of the Jews in the Persian Period'.

[5] See entry 12 above, p. 4 above.

people was served in his room. He drank a wine which he had a partiality for because of its name—*Liebfraumilch*. This name had given him the impression of something mild and light, and he drank the wine in deference to this impression, without noticing that it is in fact one of the more potent Rheinish wines!

It became a blessing to me to associate with Kierkegaard in that foreign place, because he encouraged me to do what I was beginning to think of doing, namely go back again to Denmark and try to make a place for myself there.

From Berlin I once sent Kierkegaard a cutting I found in a paper, because the Berliners' 'Ueberschwänglichkeit' (exuberance) amused him so. I sent it through our cousin Mrs. Thomsen, formerly Miss Kierkegaard.[1] Under the heading 'Enquiry', it read, 'Does it not seem appropriate that even the tinkers associate together in order to keep pace with the times?'[2] That amused Kierkegaard, for he recognized its significance.

27

After coming home from my first visit to Italy,[3] at the end of 1847, Kierkegaard came up to me one day as I stood looking in Barsugli the plasterer's shop-window in Østergade.[4] I was looking at some plaster models of antiques. We fell to talking about sculpture, and he said that previously he had really had no eye for that art, but that it was now beginning to attract him by its peacefulness. I fancy that on the whole his interest and feeling for the pictorial arts was not greatly developed. His interest in the fine arts came largely through the stimulus of poetry.

28

Shortly after the disturbances had broken out in 1848,[5] I spoke to Kierkegaard about the plan I then had to go off as a volunteer. I

[1] Mrs. Julie Augusta Thomsen, the only daughter of that Michael Andersen Kierkegaard mentioned in entry 1 above, *et passim*. She is said to be the only person who ever had a photograph of Søren Kierkegaard.

[2] 'Sollte es nicht zweckmässig seyn, dass auch die Klempner sich assoziirten, um mit dem Zeitgeiste Schritt zu halten?'

[3] Brøchner studied for a year in Berlin, beginning in April 1846 (see entry 26). From Berlin he went to Rome; that would be early in 1847. In Nov. 1847 he went back to Denmark.

[4] He lived in Store Købmagergade 7, and had his show rooms in Østergade. A plaster-cast shop in Østergade is mentioned in *Journals*, 172 (II, A, 200).

[5] Disturbances broke out in Rendsborg and Kiel, the news of which reached Copenhagen on 27 March 1848. The two duchies of Schleswig and Holstein occupy the southern half of the peninsula of Jutland, and are inhabited mostly by German-speaking people. At the time of the rising, the duchies had long been united to Denmark because their Duke was the King of Denmark; though they lived under their own laws. The Danish royal house, however, seemed like dying out on the male side. Danish law said that the crown should pass to a female line; the law of the duchies said it would fall to a secondary male line. In 1846, King Christian VIII of Denmark passed a new law, by which the unions of the duchies with Denmark was to be secured for all time. This

said that, besides the obvious call to action, I wanted to gain experience, especially self-experience. Kierkegaard agreed that this way of learning from actual life was necessary for most people, but said that he himself received a far richer reward ideally, through the media of imagination and reflection. Quite clearly this was so. He could be content with a motif from actual life, which his imagination would work out to the full, he being guided by the experience he had gained through his own ceaseless activity in the sphere of the mind.

29

Some years later I spoke with Kierkegaard on a related theme. At that time I was feeling dissatisfied that I had no fixed job and none of the fixed duties which follow from a job.[1] The complete freedom I had enjoyed in my free-lance student days was beginning to pall on me. I said to him, 'To such a degree do I miss having a definite and practical sphere of activity that I feel tempted to set up as an innkeeper, if I can find nothing else.' Kierkegaard smiled and said, 'Then you shall have my patronage.' He then went on to say that some years earlier he had received a visit from a German scholar who had probably been sent by someone or other to see this great Danish personage. He received the German very courteously, but assured him that the visit must be due to a misunderstanding somewhere. 'My brother,' he said, 'who has a German doctorate, is an extremely learned man, whom it would certainly interest you to know. But I am a beer retailer.'

30

Dr. Peter Kierkegaard once gave a course of lectures at the University. I cannot accurately remember when, but it must have been in the '50's[2] while he happened to be staying in Copenhagen.[3]

caused disaffection in the duchies, and so, encouraged by the general confusion in Europe, the Schleswig-Holsteiners revolted and boldly cast off the Danish yoke. To this day the duchies are separated from Denmark.

[1] Brøchner was at the University for nine years (1836–45). He studied abroad for one and a half years after that; lived later on grants; went on some further travels, and worked as a private tutor at the University. From 1833 he taught Greek at the school for Civic Virtue, where Kierkegaard had been a pupil (and teacher of Latin later), and not till 1857, when he was thirty-seven years old, did he get a fixed post at the University.

[2] Søren Kierkegaard's brother, mentioned in entry 1, and just now in 29. In Peter's *Journals* (unpublished) in the Royal Library, we read, 'On 7 Dec. I began, and on 11, 14, 18, 19 and 20 continued my lectures for educated people of both sexes, on Matthew 1:8–9. The first was held in the Russian's Hall(!), the others in the University's Great Hall. There was a large attendance.' (Quoted by Carl Weltzer, *Peter & Søren Kierkegaard*, p. 24, 1.) Later he published these lectures in his magazine entitled *Serials from Pedersborg*, Vol. III, and they again appear in his *Collected Works*, III (1902), pp. 24–155, under the title 'Light upon Certain Political and Ecclesiastical Questions, expounded with a detailed examination of *Matthew I*, vv. 8–9'.

[3] Peter was Rector of Pedersborg near Sorø, from 1842 to 1856, some fifty miles from Copenhagen.

They were given in the Great Hall before a large and very mixed audience. Søren Kierkegaard was quite ironical about these lectures, and with a certain element of malice he told me of a fragment of conversation he heard one evening outside the University just as the lecture was going to start. Many men, and still more women, came pouring up the steps of the University. The driver of one carriage waiting outside was accosted by a fellow passing by with the question, 'What are all these people going to do inside there?' 'Oh, they are going to a dance,' answered the driver, to the great delight of Søren Kierkegaard.

The lectures were given in the Doctor's own way, very forcibly, full of intellectuality, and in a prophetic and apocalyptic style. I could tell Søren Kierkegaard a story, *à propos* these lectures, about our old uncle in Købmagergade.[1] He went regularly to the lectures, although they went far beyond his horizon; and moreover he was very hard of hearing. He felt very proud of seeing 'his cousin's[2] son from Gammel Torv' read before such a large crowd. One evening when he arrived home from the lectures, he paced up and down the room, repeating without cessation, 'Nay, he is a unique man, this Peter Kierkegaard. How he can speak, how he can speak!' His daughter[3] ventured to ask him later, 'Could you follow his lecture? Could you hear all he said?' 'Nowt *one* word, nowt *one* word,' said the old Jutlander unsuspectingly. But his enthusiasm for the unique speaker was just as great.

31

Søren Kierkegaard once told me a funny experience he had with this uncle. The old man had a passion for making verses; but his verses made you shudder, both from their structure and content. One day he came to call on Søren Kierkegaard, and after a little introductory talk he produced a bundle of his verses, which he asked his nephew to read aloud. They sat down beside each other on the sofa. The old man leaned back and put on his spectacles in order to follow the script during the reading; doubtless also to take care that nothing was missed out. Søren Kierkegaard sat in a bending position over the papers, choosing this position so that the old man should not observe the betraying smile on his face. He read the poems from end to end with a loud voice, and with great passion. The old man was thrilled to the marrow. Tears streamed down

[1] The aforementioned Michael Andersen Kierkegaard, Brøchner's uncle.

[2] That is, Michael Pederson Kierkegaard, the father of Peter and Søren.

[3] The aforementioned Mrs. J. A. Thomsen, formerly of course Miss Kierkegaard (see entry 26). In 1845 her husband had died, and presumably she went back to live with her father, M. A. Kierkegaard.

his cheeks, so moved was he by the beautiful verses, and he left Kierkegaard with the warmest thanks.

I had often heard the verses of my old uncle. They were always remarkable, and had this wonderful quality, that with very small variations they could be used, or anyway were used, for the most heterogeneous occasions. For example, the old man had once, on the occasion of a daughter's engagement, composed a poem which was not only used then *and* for another engagement (where the personal relationship between the partners concerned was altogether different), but was also to have been used, with some quite small adaptations, on the occasion of my appointment at the University. The only reason that it was not actually used on that occasion was that the old man had not yet memorized it the evening when my appointment was announced in the *Berlingske Tidende*.[1] The announcement came a little earlier than we had expected, and we were just then having a party with the old man.

Sometimes his verses were sung, at his insistent request, by companies of friends assembled at his house. A melody was chosen which, by Procrustean methods, could somehow be made to fit the words. It was absolutely ludicrous to hear how sometimes a great many syllables had to be compressed into one mouthful, and sometimes a single syllable had to be drawn out in truly Holbergean style.[2] But to the old man's ears it all sounded the loveliest of combinations, and his face shone with the thrill of it all.

32

Old uncle Kierkegaard sometimes used the most extraordinary expressions both in writing and speaking, but chiefly in speaking. For example, when writing to his ancestral village of Sæding in Jutland about Søren Kierkegaard and his brother Peter, he used always to write 'My cousin's departed son Søren Kierkegaard,' instead of 'my departed cousin's son'. This was particularly funny in one context, when he announced his cousin's dead son Peter Kierkegaard had married again.[3] I once told Søren about this peculiarity of uncle's. It amused him; but as regards himself, he gave the words a significance quite unsuspected by the old man (who was indeed a poet inspired!) by saying that he (Søren Kierkegaard) was in truth 'as good as dead'.[4]

[1] On 6 February 1857 it was announced in the *Berlingske Tidende* that Brøchner was appointed extra-ordinary teacher in philosophy.

[2] The reference is doubtless to Harlequin's song in *The Invisible Folk*, Act II, scene 6.

[3] This Peter did on 12 June 1841.

[4] See Hebrews 11:12. In *Either/Or*, I, Søren Kierkegaard wrote several pieces addressed to his 'co-defuncts' (Sympáranekromenoi). By that time his engagement

This led him to speak of uncle's great age.[1] I said that in a sense one could not call him old, i.e. if one is to measure life's length by the amount one has done. For the old man had really 'lived' for only a very small part of the time he had existed. Most of the time he vegetated and slept. I added jokingly that Søren Kierkegaard was truly the oldest man I had known. He smiled, raising no objection to this method of computation.

33

Once Kierkegaard told me—this occurs to me here as I speak of *his* age—that when young he had gone about with the firm conviction that he would die when he was thirty-three years old. (Was it that the age of Jesus was to be the norm for his imitators?) This conviction was so rooted in him that when he passed that age he even went to look at the church register to assure himself that he was really more than thirty-three, so difficult was it for him to believe it.[2]

34

When I first began giving lectures at the University[3] Søren Kierkegaard used to speak to me about them, both about my theme (Greek philosophy) and my method of treatment. He said to me that he would some day come and hear them, but that he would not say definitely when. He never came; but the fact that I might at any time have had him for a listener made me very painstaking in handling my theme. And I verily believe that this was what Kierkegaard intended. But he would also know how nervous I should feel if he were present, and that too may have made him stay away.

35

À propos my lectures, he once discussed Aristotle's metaphysical teaching, where Aristotle defines virtue as the Mean (μεσότης)[4]

was broken: he was dead to Regine, dead to married life, dead to the world (in the sense that, as he put it, he had 'chosen the cloister', i.e. set himself to seek the inner depths of the spirit), dead in the sense that he carried a 'dead' secret about his father's sin. It was in 1839 that he first used this expression 'good as dead' about himself. He was then taking his theological examination, past the usual age for this, just as Sarah begat Isaac 'when she was past age'. See *Papirer*, II, A, 490. And see my *Kierkegaard Commentary*, Chapter VI.

1 He was ninety-one when he died on 4 Dec. 1867.

2 We may also refer to Kierkegaard's first publication (7 Sept. 1838) entitled 'From the Papers of *One Still Living*', the italicized words indicating his surprise (my own italics).

3 As unofficial lecturer, in the winter of 1849–50, Brøchner lectured on the History of Greek Philosophy. Also privately he took classes interpreting Aristotle's metaphysical teaching and Plato's *Theaetetus* and *The Sophist*.

4 This is not in the *Metaphysics* but, in the *Nicomachean Ethics*, Book II, Chapter 5. See also Brøchner's *Outline of the History of Philosophy* (1873), p. 187 f.

between two extremes. He had rightly seen that this could not apply to merit in general, but only to ethical merit. This was a point which at that time was by no means generally clear. He told me he had sought clarification of this and other points in the *Nicomachean Ethics*, from Madvig[1] and Sibbern. Madvig had said that it was a long time since he had read this work and he was no longer *au fait* with it. 'And yet Madvig is generally so reliable', added Kierkegaard. Sibbern on the other hand had immediately been able to give him the answer he sought. Kierkegaard set great store on Sibbern, though he was not blind to his weaknesses. Among these weaknesses, Kierkegaard once mentioned Sibbern's complete lack of irony; and also—this is a psychological point—his lack of perception for disguised passions, and for the way one passion takes the form of another, doubling up on it, so to speak. That was why, as Kierkegaard thought, Sibbern was so often deceived when people came to him, as many did (especially ladies), to consult him as a kind of psycho-analyst.

36

Kierkegaard often spoke of Paul Møller,[2] and always with the profoundest respect. It was Paul Møller's personality, far more that his writings, which made such an impression on him; and he used to regret that there would soon come a time when Møller's importance would no longer be appreciated, because the memory of his personality would have vanished, and only his writings would be left on which to base judgement. Kierkegaard once told me a funny anecdote about Møller. He was to 'oppose' *ex officio* a thesis, and had jotted down his notes on loose pieces of paper which he slipped between the pages of his copy of the thesis. He introduced each of his objections with the words, 'graviter vituperandum est'[3] ('it must be seriously

[1] J. N. Madvig (1804–86), Professor of Philosophy, especially for Latin language and literature.

[2] Paul Martin Møller (1794–1838). Born in Uldum near Vejle in Jutland, he came up to Copenhagen University in 1812, and thereafter began life as an author. But suddenly he left Copenhagen to become chaplain of a ship to China; partly in order to get quiet and come to terms with himself. On his return he soon became a *persona grata* with the Students' Union. Under Sibbern's influence he turned to the study of philosophy, and in 1826 he was appointed Lector, then in 1828 Professor, of Philosophy. His poem *Joy over Denmark* is still much beloved. It is referred to in the introduction to Kierkegaard's *Concept of Dread.* Kierkegaard attended his lectures and was greatly drawn to him. Møller was about the only lecturer who really understood Kierkegaard. When he lay dying, Møller sent to Kierkegaard a message through Professor Sibbern, 'Tell Kierkegaard not to undertake too much. Doing so has damaged me.' Kierkegaard was then projecting a full-scale philosophical work in the manner of Hegel. He gave it up and turned to the study of irony, a theme suggested to him by P. M. Møller. When Kierkegaard in 1835–6 wrote four anonymous articles in the *Flying Post*, Møller wrote and congratulated Heiberg, thinking Heiberg the author! We learn from Hertz's diary that on 4 June a party was held at the Heibergs' with Møller present. It was after this party that Kierkegaard, who had been the soul of wit, went home and wanted to shoot himself. See *Journals*, 53 (I, A, 161).

[3] The disputating for doctors' degrees was always carried on in Latin. The incident

objected that . . .'). When the candidate had given his answer, Møller replied very pleasantly 'concedo' ('I yield') and went on to the next objection. After quite a short time Møller concluded his opposition with an apology that he had no more time to go on with this interesting discussion, and as he was departing he passed Kierkegaard among the listeners. In a half-voice he said to Kierkegaard, 'Shall we go to Pleish's?'[1] (the coffee house he used to frequent). During the examination all Møller's notes had fallen out of the book and fluttered around on the floor, and the audience had been amused to see the great figure Møller crawling about picking up the scattered papers.

37

A man with whom I used frequently to see Kierkegaard walking in these years was Professor Kolderup-Rosenvinge.[2] I suppose their common interest in aesthetic matters drew them together. Kolderup-Rosenvinge was a cultured man who had made a special study of South European literature, and had translated something of Calderon, but he was rather dull and in many ways extremely narrow-minded. When I once expressed my surprise to Kierkegaard that he found any interest in talking with Rosenvinge, he emphasized Rosenvinge's wide culture. Kierkegaard used to rate highly people of an elder generation who preserved an old-time interest in culture and possessed a gentility of manner which our younger generation so much lacked.

38

Kierkegaard had for a long time (in the years 1841–45) associated much with the late Pastor Spang.[3] He would fetch Spang from his home almost every day for a fairly long evening walk (several

here referred to was at the disputation for a doctorate on 25 Oct. 1836. The candidate was F. O. Lange, later a headmaster and titular professor.

[1] A coffee house on Amagertorv 4.

[2] J. L. Kolderup-Rosenvinge (1792–1850). There is a series of letters between him and Kierkegaard, published in *Breve og Aktstykker*, I, p. 196 ff. They were first published in *Det Danske Tidsskrift* for 1898, pp. 69–102, by the very F. O. Lange mentioned in section 36. Brøchner's judgement that Kolderup-Rosenvinge was dull and narrow-minded is certainly not borne out by these letters.

[3] P. J. Spang (1796–1846) was curate (1840), and then parish-priest (1845) of the Church of the Holy Spirit, where Kierkegaard had been baptized. In 1844, Kierkegaard wrote, 'Today Spang went into the pulpit with great assurance and unction, and gesticulated far and wide' (*Papirer*, V, A, 17). This was probably on the 12 May. See also *Postscript*, p. 436 (VII, p. 477) for a note on gesticulating clergymen. In X, A, 149 (1849), Kierkegaard writes, 'The late Spang once told me he had had some of his most glorious moments in the pulpit. Well, such feelings, and such power of imagination, have some artistic value perhaps. But may not an actor speak in the same way?' Writing in 1846, Kierkegaard says, 'My service of the Idea [i.e. Truth] is my highest interest; it is the goal of my effort in all my art. This is something I thought (but only quite dimly), that I might initiate Spang into' (*Papirer*, VII, A, 105). On a loose bit of paper Kierkegaard once wrote (1847–8), 'I must dedicate some little book or other to the departed Spang' (*Papirer*, VIII^1, A, 658).

interesting letters to Spang from Søren Kierkegaard are in the possession of his daughter, Mrs. Rump).[1] After Spang was dead, Kierkegaard once told me how his widow had been overwhelmed with sorrow, and how he had helped to calm her mind by speaking to her.[2] He then used this phrase, 'I know how one has to mourn, and I also know how one ought to be comforted in sorrow.' And he certainly did understand as very few did. His way of comforting was not to cover up the sorrow, but to bring it right out into the open, and then remind the sorrowful one that if it was a *duty* to mourn, it was also for that very reason a duty not to let oneself be weighed down by grief, but in the grief to keep up one's strength for one's work; yes, even to find an inducement to do one's work better.

I myself have more than once learnt from experience how Kierkegaard understood the art of lifting one up when one felt bowed down; of comforting when one was worried—and this without your having to tell him what was weighing on you or upsetting you. I remember for example that in the autumn of 1850 I had to live for a short time in a boarding house, because I could not find a flat at the right moment. Under pressure of circumstances, despondent thoughts were getting the upper hand of me. One evening, while I was walking in the street all out of spirits, I met Kierkegaard who began a conversation. Without my needing to say a word, he saw with his sharp glance that I longed to be lifted out of this despondent mood; and he knew, without seeming for a moment to refer to my trouble directly, how to set my heart at liberty. I left him happy and confident, and was for a long time freed from the power of depression.

39

Much of what Kierkegaard has given us in his writings he touched upon, I remember, in talks with me while his thoughts were working upon it. The fact that it was still in embryo gave it an even fuller and larger life than it had when fully formed. I remember, for example, that when he was with Christens[3] and myself he brought forward a theme he has often treated in his *Edifying Discourses*, that 'all life is a time of trial'. His argument was that for a believer there is an 'at last' which seems to be so near that it can be seized

[1] Two letters are printed in *Breve og Aktstykke*, Nos. 51 and 61.

[2] See *E.P.*, II, p. 871, where Spang's son says, 'For a long time after my father's death Kierkegaard would often come to see us. After speaking to us all, he would go alone with mother into a room where they could sit quietly, and where he could speak comfortingly to her. We could well see with what blessing he must have spoken to her in these quiet times; we observed how she benefited, and how she longed for him when he was absent longer than usual. He was in the best sense of the word a friend and consolation to the widow.'

[3] See note 3 to section 6.

upon. But it constantly recedes; and only at life's ending are we *made* to seize it. Only in death can one say 'at last'.[1]

Sometimes Kierkegaard expressed himself in conversation in a more pointed, more paradoxical form than in his writings. It pleased him to formulate his thoughts in such a way that they expressed the very opposite of what was generally accepted. In contradistinction to the phrase 'experience makes one wise', he used to propound the thesis 'experience makes one mad'. And he would adduce his proofs with much piquancy, by pointing to all the innumerable contradistinctions in concrete experience.

40

The difference between Kierkegaard and myself in spiritual life and outlook, and in our basically different attitudes towards Christianity, came into definite purview from time to time when we conversed together. Once—I think it must have been in 1851—he asked me what work I was engaged upon at the moment. I answered that I was reading the New Testament. That seemed to please him; but he was not pleased when I added that I read it only with the specific purpose of finding primitive Christianity, in order thereafter to trace the successive developments of dogmatic positions in Christian tradition. For him such research was almost offensive. Although in his writings he refers to doctrine very little, and generally limits himself to what is central in Christianity, he could not treat Scripture as an object for critical research, partly because Scripture was for him a unity—a coherent whole expressing Christianity—into which he would introduce no cleavage, and partly because by making Scripture an object of scientific study you made it an object of knowledge, instead of an object of faith.

41

I never concealed from Kierkegaard my divergence from him in my attitude towards Christianity. But we never argued about this.[2] There was so much on which we felt at one that I preferred to try and learn from him all I could (and there was a great deal that was of deep significance to me), rather than enter into arguments. He could certainly, through his superior talent, have easily overwhelmed me; but he could not easily have convinced me. His attitude in our

[1] See *Edifying Discourses*, I, p. 32 (III, p. 41), IV, p. 72 (V, p. 135); *Training in Christianity*, p. 193 (XII, p. 218). The first hint of this thought coming to Kierkegaard is in *Papirer*, II, A, 561: 'The words "at last" which appear in all our collects are like an epic, charged with Fate; but if they are thought of lyrically, they are quite insufferable. They are the true Christian password to the solution of difficulties.'

[2] Probably because Kierkegaard knew that it is no use arguing. The Christian can only witness, and that I think is what Brøchner's word 'reporting' really means.

talks was essentially that of someone reporting to me; and I recognized in this a proof of his good will towards me. He had two methods of conversation. One was essentially a reporting, meant to rouse and stimulate. The other was essentially an ironic questioning, meant to confound through its dialectic. He never used this latter method with me. Occasionally when I became animated, he would put in a mischievous and teasing word. For example, I once said with much animation that no positive religion could be tolerant, because by asserting itself to be a revealed religion it was obliged to claim to be the only true religion, all the others being regarded as false. A general religion, a 'religion-in-general', must therefore from a positive religion's point of view be a non-entity. While I was saying all this with animation, I repeated the expression, 'religion-in-general', and made the statement that for me a religion, i.e. a *positive* religion, was in general a non-entity. 'Yes, but confound your "in general",' said Kierkegaard,[1] and damped my zeal. It is, however, the only teasing of that sort I remember from him.

If he never tried directly to oppose my diverging views, I can only conclude from the friendly sympathy he always showed me (which I remember gratefully) that it was because he realized that I honestly and seriously occupied myself with that thing he regarded as the highest.[2] He knew that I was so familiar with what he had written about it (and indeed with his whole teaching) that I had sufficient premises for my conclusions. I would not be led to Christianity by another, but, whatever happened, only by myself.[3]

42

On the general effect of Søren Kierkegaard's writings, I once said something which seemed to make some impression on him. He was saying that as an author he had had the peculiar fate of publishing one book after another without provoking any real criticism,[4] for or against. He declared that from the start his books had found a steady circle of readers, since the number of copies sold straight away was always about the same—seventy in each case, not including *Either/Or*.[5] I expressed my conviction that quite a considerable

[1] Kierkegaard uses a phrase from Holberg with a derisive play upon words which cannot be reproduced in English.

[2] Christianity.

[3] I suspect that while this is perfectly true as far as it goes, Kierkegaard realized the futility of mere argument, and preferred to witness.

[4] Evidently Kierkegaard did not think much of the criticisms that *had* come out!—e.g. by Heiberg (1843), Hagen (1845), Liunges, Kofoed-Hansen, and others (to mention only the earlier criticisms). See Aage Kabell, *Kierkegaardstudiet i Norden*, p. 49 ff.

[5] This is only those sold 'straight away'. In *Søren Kierkegaard og Pengene*, by Brandt and Rammel (p. 18), a list of sales is given up to 1847. Ten books had been

number of people read his books, and with real seriousness. The silence of the press, I thought, was largely due to the critics' feeling that his writings were beyond their criticisms. Silence was by no means a sign of the general public's indifference, and I thought he had already influenced the public on a large scale. I added that in my judgement the effect of his writings, as regards Christianity, had been as much negative as positive. All who had been influenced by his writings, in one direction or the other, were certainly agreed that Christianity, as he conceived it, had a real character of its own, and inculcated respect. But his way of defining Christianity was such that it was bound to put many off, as was the case with me.[1] and it did so because of the separation it postulated between Christianity and nature, and Christianity and concrete life.[2]

I was saying all this just as we were taking leave of each other. He became silent and gave me his hand. He left me in silence, but he had a friendly expression on his face.

43

Kierkegaard expressed himself without reserve on the significance his writings may have had for certain persons. His old uncle, M. Kierkegaard the merchant, had a son a few years younger than Søren Kierkegaard. This son was a cripple, paralysed all down one side, and completely deformed in body,[3] but intellectually very talented. He read his cousin's Søren Kierkegaard's writings with great interest, visited Kierkegaard from time to time in his home, and received much spiritual uplift from these visits. I once spoke to Søren Kierkegaard about him, and told him how greatly the lad had been impressed by one of Kierkegaard's works, namely the discourse for a Confession-Service[4] in *Edifying Discourses in Different Vein.*

published to date, and the number sold was 2,396, or an average of 239·6 for each book. (*Either/Or*'s 525 copies were sold out and a second edition came later). Later books sold even better.

[1] And with Christ himself. 'He that is not with me is against me,' said Jesus, and, 'Blessed is he that is not offended in me' (Matthew 12:30, and 11:6).

[2] It is often said that Kierkegaard made this separation. In a sense he did. He felt that for him, natural science would have been an unsatisfactory study, because it deals solely with the phenomenal (see *Journals*, 16 = I, A, 72). How many English natural scientists today are themselves warning us that their studies are quite incomplete without the spiritual as basis. And if Kierkegaard seems to belittle the concrete too much, is it not because most people stress it too much? To be a 'realist' today often means to work for the betterment of concrete life. Nowhere has concrete life been more uplifted than by Christianity, and in Christendom. But is concrete the final 'reality'? Kierkegaard is concerned to stress that the 'real' is the spiritual and the eternal, not the concrete. Our age sorely needs this emphasis today!

[3] See section 2, note 1.

[4] Entitled *Purify your Hearts* in the English translation by Aldworth and Ferrie (referred to in note 3) and *Purity of Heart* in the American translation by Douglas Steere.

(In it Kierkegaard speaks of a man who, through bodily infirmity, is prevented from fulfilling an outward task. Beautifully and upliftingly it is said how such a man still retains his ordinary ethical task unimpaired, and that his life's work merely takes on a special form.[1]) Kierkegaard said, 'Yes, for him the passage is a blessing'; and that was indeed true. It had the power to give this sorely tried man strength to overcome the thought that his life was useless and wasted, and to make him feel that he really was the equal of those more fortunately endowed by Nature. It was precisely Kierkegaard's lively ability to make him feel like this that made him go away from the above-mentioned conversations with Kierkegaard with renewed strength.

44

I have often recalled a conversation I had with Søren Kierkegaard a short time before his *Training in Christianity* came out.[2] We were walking together by the Lakes,[3] and he was calling upon me not to put off beginning to publish something. He added jokingly, 'There is now a vacant place in our literature. *I have finished*.' This statement, which went over me lightly, came vividly to my mind when the last part of Kierkegaard's authorship was concluded. When he spoke thus to me, he was obviously still nourishing the hope of being able to avoid his last attack against the Establishment. If this had not been forced upon him, his authorship would have been essentially concluded when *Training* took its place among his writings. For truly all the stages which he had had to go through were at that time passed. His writings formed a wonderfully rounded whole.[4] But the last stage carries in itself the possibility of re-statement, and the possibility became actuality when someone tried to reduce his conception of Christianity to an eccentric exaggeration, and to make mediocrity and insipidity the real norm.[5]

[1] See *Purify Your Hearts*, p. 133 f. (VIII, p. 242 f.).

[2] 27 Sept. 1850.

[3] A series of four large natural lakes, which in Kierkegaard's day stood outside the old city, on its western side, in rural beauty. They are now well within the modern city, but are still very beautiful, and crowded with wild-fowl of many kinds.

[4] There were in fact four more books after *Training*, published in Brøchner's lifetime, the last quite a big one. They are: (i) An *Edifying Discourse* entitled 'The Woman that was a Sinner' (20 Dec. 1850); (ii) *Two Discourses for Communion on Fridays* (7 Aug. 1851); (iii) *On my work as author* (7 Aug. 1851); and (iv) *For Self-Examination* (12 Sept. 1851). Two further works, one published the year after Brøchner died, are: (i) *Point of View*, written 1848, published by Peter Kierkegaard 1859; (ii) *Judge for Yourself* (written 1851–2), also published by Kierkegaard's brother Peter in 1876.

[5] Brøchner is probably thinking of Martensen's *Dogmatic Explanations* (1850) where M. protests strongly against S.K.'s conception of faith as passion. M. cannot regard that sort of Christianity as normal.

45

In the same conversation, Kierkegaard went on to emphasize one side of his authorship, which he spoke of with characteristic objectivity. I mean the significance his writings had for Danish prose. He said, 'Our literature in this century has shown an almost abnormal richness in poetry; our prose, on the contrary, has declined.' We lacked, he said, a prose which bore the stamp of artistry. 'This lack I have supplied, and that is why my writings will retain their importance in our literature.' I am sure he was right. His prose is an art, not indeed without its clouds, but as a whole the clearest, most pliable, richest in compass, and most satisfying that our literature knows, both for expressing the thought and (not less) for expressing feeling and passion. It often reminds me of Plato, the author whose prose I would most of all compare with Kierkegaard's. Plato was certainly Kierkegaard's model, and he shaped his art after him, though with due freedom.

46

Kierkegaard expressed himself many times about Grundtvig and Grundtvigianism,[1] and nearly always saw its funny side. He often spoke in a similar way in conversation. The sharp contrast between his own conception of religion and the Grundtvigian was constantly in evidence; and the childlike spontaneity of Grundtvig looks comic by the contrast. Only about one period of Grundtvig's life did Kierkegaard once speak to me with any interest and approval, and that was about the particular period when Grundtvig attacked Clausen.[2] But what attracted Kierkegaard about this attack was clearly nothing specifically Grundtvigian, least of all Grundtvig's 'matchless discovery'[3] (which always struck Kierkegaard as 'matchless nonsense' and unoriginal nonsense at that) but its emphasis upon what really stands opposed to Rationalism, namely change in a man's *life*. Søren Kierkegaard's father, whose religion was pretty much that of the old pietists, sympathized with Grundtvig and Lindberg,[4] I suppose from this antirationalist point of view. Søren

[1] See, e.g. *Postscript*, p. 36 ff. (VII, p. 27 ff.). Cf. *Papirer*, II, A, 300, and Carl Weltzer's *Grundtvig and Kierkegaard.*

[2] H. N. Clausen (1793–1877), Professor in Theology 1822–1877. In 1825 appeared his *The Doctrines, Ritual, and Church-theory of Catholicism and Protestantism.* This Grundtvig stamped as rationalism, and a falsifying of Christianity. A bitter strife ensued.

[3] Namely that it was in the Church rather than in the Bible that truth is conserved. This is one of Grundtvig's main tenets. See *Postscript*, *loc. cit.*

[4] J. C. Lindberg (1797–1857), a follower of Grundtvig from his undergraduate days. He published various theological magazines in which he attacked Clausen bitterly. His modern translation of the Bible (completed by his son) is still used by the Grundtvigians.

Kierkegaard's sympathy had undoubtedly the same motive and the same limits as his father's.

47

Speaking of Grundtvig, I am reminded of a little trait of Søren Kierkegaard. The Queen-mother Caroline Amalie,[1] patroness of Grundtvigianism, esteemed Kierkegaard greatly, at any rate before his attack on Mynster. Søren Kierkegaard was by no means insusceptible to any goodwill shown him by a queen. One day I was walking with him along Love-lane[2] when he suddenly cried, 'Oh damn! Now I cannot escape.' I looked at him in surprise, for he was not given to swearing. Then I looked in front of us along the lane, and saw a long way off a red-coated servant and before him two ladies. One of these was the Queen-mother, and when we met her, she very graciously stopped Kierkegaard and talked to him. When we first saw her we were so far away that we could easily have turned round without being noticed. That his outburst was not altogether sincere was, I felt, indicated by that 'Oh, damn!' It was not like him, and it sounded a little forced. We often conceal our entire satisfaction at something that is happening by using strong language! Søren Kierkegaard's old-world, traditional respect for royalty was not without its significance where the Queen-mother was concerned.

48

In the autumn of 1852 I had a talk with Kierkegaard about Bishop Mynster. How often have I recalled this since Kierkegaard took up cudgels against him! I was walking one afternoon along the ramparts, on the path up by the parapet, and there I passed Bishop Mynster. A moment later I met Søren Kierkegaard, who was descending the ramparts. He beckoned to me to join him. He had seen Mynster walking in front of him, and we fell to talking about him. Kierkegaard spoke first of Mynster's stately and noble exterior; then of his wise and genteel appearance. He said that as a man of the world, Mynster was superior to most of our younger men. These had for a long time thought that with their philosophic equipment they could treat Mynster like an inferior; but upon personal acquaintance they were soon overcome by him and submitted to him.

[1] Both King Christian VIII and Queen Caroline Amalie set great store by Søren Kierkegaard. See *Journals*, 743, 867, 868, 869, 1074, for Kierkegaard's conversations with Christian VIII. In 868 the Queen is mentioned. She called *Either/Or*, 'Either and Or'!

[2] One of the walks along the Lakes mentioned in section 44, note 3. These walks were called Love Lane, Friendship Lane, and Marriage Lane respectively. It is perhaps sad they are now entirely renamed and have become modern boulevards.

He mentioned Martensen as one who, with his usual clumsiness and lack of *finesse*, had treated Mynster with a great deal of haughtiness.

But Kierkegaard emphasized very strongly that Mynster's power lay in his worldly wisdom, and that this was the deciding factor in all he did. Kierkegaard spoke very ironically about his own relationship to Mynster. He told me with a smile that he had once requested Mynster's permission to seek his Right Reverence's guidance when he had problems which he could not clarify by himself. And Mynster had given his permission. The smile alone with which he said this showed me clearly how little worth he really put upon Mynster at that time. And the whole way in which he characterized Mynster as 'a man of the world' was in full accord with his later statements. There was a time when he thought very highly of Mynster,[1] but this was really due to respect for his own father, who set great store by Mynster. This pious respect for his father's judgements I saw in many contexts. It often decided Kierkegaard's own attitude. I remember for example he once of his own free will talked to me about a man who in no way deserved respect and who, as a person, could not possibly have inspired Kierkegaard's interest. But Kierkegaard's father felt great esteem and gratitude towards this man, because his wise advice had once prevented the father's monetary affairs from getting into disorder. It was when financial crisis threatened Denmark after the war with England.[2]

49

At the time when Søren Kierkegaard began his polemic against the Establishment,[3] and perhaps for some time before, he had ceased to participate in church services. Before that he had been a very regular worshipper. The late Dr. Frederick Beck[4] once told me that at the time of the attack Søren Kierkegaard usually visited the Athenæum[5] on Sunday mornings during church time. Dr. Beck, with his characteristic love of sarcastic remarks, interpreted this as meaning that Kierkegaard wanted to draw people's attention to the fact that he was not in church.

[1] Previously to about 1848, when his idea changed. The world knew nothing of this, however, until the attack on Mynster came in 1854, and everybody was surprised, because outwardly Kierkegaard had been respectful.

[2] The State banks became insolvent in 1813, but Søren Kierkegaard's father had put his money in investments which were not affected thereby.

[3] i.e. in December 1854.

[4] A. F. Beck (1816–61), philosopher and theologian. He was much influenced by Strauss, as was Brøchner. He reviewed Kierkegaard's M.A. thesis, *The Concept of Irony*. See *S.V.*, XIII, p. 436, and especially p. 439 ff., where Kierkegaard pokes fun at him for saying 'the majority cannot understand the book'.

[5] A reading club, founded about 1832.

Many years earlier Kierkegaard had once asked me whether I went to church. I said no, and explained my absence as due partly to the fact that I felt a stranger there, and partly because there were so many distractions during the services in the Copenhagen churches. I said that I could never maintain a feeling of devotion. Rather I was offended. To that he replied that it was our *duty* not to let ourselves be disturbed by what went on around us. One *ought* to be uplifted when one was in church.

50

The last time I talked to Søren Kierkegaard was in the summer of 1855.[1] I had not seen him for an unusually long time. It was one evening when I was walking from Højbroplads to Vimmelskaftet. After speaking a little about my short-lived participation in political life (I had been a Member of Parliament in the winter 1854–5),[2] we soon fell to talking about his polemic against the Established Church. I thanked him warmly for what he was doing, and said how many I had come across who inwardly sympathized with him. He spoke with the greatest clarity and calm of the situation he had evoked; and it surprised me that in the midst of such a violent struggle, which encroached into his life so deeply, and took its toll of his last powers, he could maintain not only his calm and confidence, but could also preserve his wit. As we approached his home in Klædeboderne,[3] he said to me in a joking tone, 'Now I am going home and going to rest, and so I say to the world what a certain "Kammerraad"[4] said.' I asked him what this was. He replied by telling me of a queer person who once lived in his street. He was a Kammerraad by title, and regularly, every evening, carried on the following conversation with the town watchman. When the watch had called 'Ten o'clock', the Kammerraad opened his window and asked, 'Watchman, what time is it?' 'Ten o'clock, Hr. Kammerraad.' 'Good! then I think I will go to bed. If anyone enquires for me, you can ask them to lick my bottom.'[5]

He told me this story with his usual twinkle and I said good-night, not suspecting that I had spoken to him for the last time.

[1] Kierkegaard died on 11 Nov. 1855. His attack on the Church was in full swing for the previous ten or eleven months. It began with an article in the *Fatherland*, 18 Dec. 1854.

[2] He was member for Fredericia, his native town.

[3] Part of what is now Skindergade (Skinners St.), No. 38.

[4] Literally 'councillor of the chamber', a purely titular office, like M.B.E., say. There is no exact English equivalent.

[5] The last four words were omitted in the first published text of 1877 in *The Nineteenth Century*, where Brandts has written instead ('Gøtz von Berlichingen's reply'). This refers to Goethe's play of that name, where Gøtz says of someone he despises, 'He can lick, etc.' Kierkegaard gives the story he here tells to Brøchner, in *Papirer*, VIII, A, 412, under the heading 'The Joy of Living'!

TWO LETTERS FROM BRØCHNER TO C. K. F. MOLBECH

Brøchner (see p. 4) bequeathed all his papers, including the *Recollections*, to C. K. F. Molbech. Molbech (1821–88) was a poet, and a close friend of Brøchner's. Together they produced (with C. Ploug also helping) the comedy mentioned in extract 11, note 1 above, which was directed against Heiberg. In 1853 Molbech took the post of Professor of Danish and Norsk Literature at Kiel. Hence this correspondence. He remained at Kiel till the war of 1864, when Denmark lost so much to the Germans. His chief work was a translation of Dante into Danish. Both he and Brøchner loved Italy, where they had lived together as students.

Brøchner was a help to Molbech in the translation, and Molbech was a comfort and stay to Brøchner in his Italian love affair (see p. 3). Both thought along the same free-thinking, monistic lines.

Letter dated 2nd December 1855 from Copenhagen[1]

You can imagine that Søren Kierkegaard's death[2] is an event which has caused a stir among people—a thing he would not at all like. Upon me, his death has had a painful, but by no means depressing, effect. He had meant a great deal to me, both in his writings and in our personal relationship. There is no one whose personality has inspired and stimulated me to such an extent as his. The friendly disposition he always showed towards me often gave me courage when I was in danger of losing it. I remember with joy how over the long period I knew him—about twenty years in all—his gentleness and lovableness always outweighed the strong ironic and polemic element in his nature; and how his thought gradually increased in richness, certainty and clarity. A word from him would often have a soothing and reconciling effect, and clear up a confusion which one could not cope with in one's own strength. I shall certainly miss him. But when I think how completely he has fulfilled his life's mission, how rich and copious that life was in its short duration, and how much of him is left behind, I cannot think of his death with any feeling of depression. On the contrary his death

[1] See Hans Brøchner and Chr. K. F. Molbech, *En Brevvexling*, published with an Introduction by Harald Høffding, Gyldendal, 1902, p. 174.
[2] 11 Nov. 1855, three weeks before this letter was written.

seems to me beautiful and felicitous. I have received from my cousin an exquisite little portrait of him; a pencil-sketch which was made when he was in his twenty-fifth year.[1] Although he changed considerably after that time, one gets a very vivid idea of him, for the sketch is characteristically conceived.

Letter dated 17th February 1856 from Copenhagen[2]

I am really somewhat puzzled how to answer your letter. For what can I tell you about Kierkegaard's life and personality which is both interesting and new to you? Of his life there is very little to say, if one keeps to external circumstances. That he was born the 5 May 1813; that he entered the University in 1830 and took his degree in 1840, became Magister in 1841, and died in 1855—these are about all the external biographical data that can be adduced, and they are not interesting. So much the richer I suppose was his inner life and his personal development. But that has made its mark upon his writings; and its best content is set down therein. I am not really able to tell you about the beginnings of his personal development. When I first got to know him, he was already mature, I quite young. I tried at that time to understand him just as he was, without venturing to inquire how he had become so. Only later, by continual study of his writings, did I get any idea of the way he had developed; and I never sought to confirm this personally. The predominant influence in his childhood was religion; and that in a strictly orthodox form. This formed the basic strain in his life. Living with his father and his elder brother developed in him that sharp dialectic which in his youth ran away with him, so to say, and in his later years became an instrument for his religious advancement. From the time he began to study independently, it was German philosophy and poetry that specially influenced him. Hegelian philosophy occupied him for a long time; even, it would seem, overwhelmed him. But his respect for the ethical demands of existence taught him at length to see the fallacy of Hegelian philosophy.

[1] Two pencil sketches were made by Søren Kierkegaard's cousin, Christopher Kierkegaard, for another cousin, Julie Kierkegaard. They were made in 1838, i.e. in Søren Kierkegaard's twenty-fifth year. Brøchner therefore must be referring to one of them. Lowrie tells us (see *Point of View*, beginning) that Julie Kierkegaard, who became Mrs. Thomsen, had a son who treasured at any rate one of these portraits; and that this man's nephew, Mr. Ruby Thomsen, had a plaster relief, which Lowrie thinks was made from the said sketch, or perhaps from a photograph of it. See also Henriette's *Recollections*, extract 1.

[2] Hans Brøchner and C. K. F. Molbech, *En Brevvexling*, p. 186.

Besides Hegel, he was also influenced by Lessing, Hamann, Jacobi, and Kant; and later by the study of the Greeks. Among the latter, Socrates, whom he regarded with the reverence due to a genius, always stood out for him as the *human* ideal. The romantic school in Germany was of importance to him too, for its philosophers and its poets. Friedrich Schlegel's *Lucinde* suggested many an idea to him, as we see from his M.A. thesis on Irony, and the first part of *Either/Or*. But the strains from it are no mere echoes. There sounds a deeper note throughout. He also followed the course of our own Danish poetry with the most lively interest, and with a piety which often led him to over-valuation. Heiberg's *Flying Post* and the aesthetic quarrels of the time contributed to the development of his own aesthetic theories.

He always held aloof from active participation in practical politics. But as a young man he interested himself in political *theory* not a little; and in the old days he was Lehmann's[1] steadfast opponent in the Students' Union, when Lehmann was fighting for the liberal view. Kierkegaard was brought up to the strictly conservative view; and later on the whole trend of his life led him to a decided dislike of all attempts to change the outward order.

His personality you know as well as I do, except that my recollection goes a little further back. But you knew him, of course, while he was still young, when he boldly and polemically fought with the sharp weapons of dialectic and irony for poetical ideals against what was prosaic and maudlin. You will remember him too in his elder years, when, with a high standard ever before his eyes, he worked 'in the service of the Divine'; doing so with an energy of will which would not be cowed by his weakness of body, and which compressed into a few short years what ordinarily would be contained in a long and rich life. You will have retained, as perfectly as I have, a picture of this life. It was characterized by an artistry wherein everything was given over to the service of the Idea[2]; where everything was subordinated to its sovereignty, in obvious harmony. Only in his latest days have you been unable to form a picture of him.[3] But I know that in his earnest conflict with the Church, when 'his wish was death, his longing the grave, his desire that this wish and this longing might soon be fulfilled', he maintained his loving sympathy for others, even down to the smallest things in life; maintained his gentleness and friendliness, even his sense of fun; maintained his

[1] P. M. Orla Lehmann (1810–70). The 'July revolution' of 1830, when Charles X of France was deposed, and Ludvig Philip's rule began, putting an end to absolutism, made Lehmann turn to the Liberal movement, of which he became a protagonist. He was the editor of the liberal paper the *Fatherland*. See p. 43, note 2.

[2] A Hegelian term meaning 'the totality of Truth'.

[3] Molbech left Copenhagen for Kiel two years before Kierkegaard died.

equanimity and clarity of thought; above all, maintained, through faith, a peacefulness and repose which did not desert him, even in the terrible sufferings of his death-bed.

You will be able to complete this picture from your own recollections. One thing will I add, which can hardly be known to you. You know that there has been much talk of Kierkegaard's great fortune, and he has been upbraided because, by possessing it, he was really contradicting his own teaching. The day he was taken to hospital, he sent 300 dollars[1] to Gjødvad,[2] to pay off some small debts, and also to pay for his stay in hospital. These 300 dollars were the last remains of his fortune. From them the hospital bill could just be paid, but there was not enough for the cost of the funeral. That was his 'great fortune'. He left behind him only his books and a poor lot of furniture. He must have given the greater part of his fortune away,[3] for he never spent any significant part of it on himself, except during the years when his work as an author was most strenuous, and demanded support in order to put him in the right mood.

You ask me to give you the main points to which his last conflict was directed. They can really be summed up in one. He was set against the amalgamation of worldliness and Christianity. For him Christianity was something completely heterogeneous to the world. Christianity is absurd to the intellect, and can only be appropriated through the passion of faith. It demands that we die to the world; its hallmark is suffering; its constant attendant is the possibility of causing offence. So he directed his polemic against everything which rested securely in an unspiritual amalgamation of Christianity and worldliness; against every presentation of Christianity as something we are born into without ado, by birth or by ceremonies; against every attempt to treat falsely a religion whose aim ought to be to transform life, by making it merely an object of thought, or of poetical presentation.

That is the real content of his last polemic. The rest you will find in my article to the *Fatherland* which I will send you tomorrow, for I do not possess a copy myself!

Take pot-luck with these poor jottings which I have put together while rather tired and sleepy. Goodness knows whether any good

[1] About £30, worth some £120 today.

[2] F. J. Gjødvad (1811–91), secretary to the *Fatherland.* He came early under the influence of Liberalism, and was a friend of Lehmann. He gave up his career as a jurist, to fight, through journalism, for the cause of freedom. The *Fatherland* was a daily newspaper which he helped to found, and to which he was the chief contributor. He was a friend of Kierkegaard, and as a young man K. wrote many articles for the paper. These are printed in *Samlede Værker*, XIII, *passim.*

[3] Fr. Brandt and E. Rammel, in *Søren Kierkegaard and his Money* (1935), make out that this is not so.

will come of *Either/Or* coming out in German.[1] If any particular work of Kierkegaard is to be translated it ought to be the *Unscientific Postscript*. All the other work (i.e. *Either/Or*) will easily be misunderstood, since it is only a fragment.[2]

[1] It is interesting that *Either/or* had been translated as early as 1856.

[2] How true this is, and how many have been misled by reading *Either/Or* and thinking it is Kierkegaard's last views. It is in fact a brilliant presentation of the aesthetic life, which he discarded.

HENRIETTE LUND

Part II

HENRIETTE LUND'S RECOLLECTIONS OF KIERKEGAARD

INTRODUCTORY NOTE

Henriette Lund (1829–1909) was Søren Kierkegaard's niece. Her mother (1801–34) was Søren Kierkegaard's eldest sister Petrea. Her father was Ferdinand Lund (1803–75), manager of the National Bank.

Ferdinand had two brothers. Christian Lund (1799–1875), merchant, town councillor and member of the consultative chamber. He married Søren Kierkegaard's eldest sister, Nicoline (1799–1832). After his wife's death he remained a widower for forty-three years (see extract 8), and continued to live in Kobmagergade. He is Henriette's 'Uncle Christian' and his children are her cousins, Sophie, Henrich, and Michael—all referred to in her *Recollections.*

The other brother was Vilhelm Lund (1801–80), a naturalist. From 1832 till his death he lived at Lagoa Santa in Brazil. Kierkegaard as a young man wrote a letter to him there. See *Journals*, 16 (I, A, 72). This letter is important for its discussion of Kierkegaard's own career (see page 59).

Henriette was the eldest child of Petrea and Ferdinand Lund. There were also three boys. Vilhelm (1831–1902) who was given the honorific title of 'Councillor', owned the large farm called 'Annisegaard' in North Sjælland, where these *Recollections* were written. Then Christian (1833–1904), the owner of Bregningegaard in N.W. Sjælland, and Peter (1834–64), who took an M.A. in theology and was destined for the priesthood. He volunteered in the war with Germany in 1864 and was killed at Dybbøl Bjerg.

After the death of Petrea, Ferdinand married his cousin Catherine Lund (1800–59). There were three sons of this second marriage —half-brothers to Henriette. The one that chiefly concerns this book is Troels Lund (1840–1921), who became an historian. In his writings he tells us much about his Uncle Søren—in Vol. III of *Bakkehus and Solbjerg* and in *Et Liv.* Extracts from the latter are given in Part III, Section IV.

Henriette wrote these *Recollections* at 'Annisegaard', the home of her brother Vilhelm, partly in January 1876 and partly in September 1876. They were first printed privately, for relations and friends only. But the first edition was soon sold out, and Henriette was asked for a public edition. She did not wish this, but decided that the work should be published after her death. She died in May 1909, in her eightieth year, and the *Recollections* were then published openly.

'Annisegaard', where Henriette wrote, is a lovely farm on the shores of Lake Arre (in Danish Arresø). Descendants of the family still occupy the place, and I treasure my copy of the *Recollections* because it was given to me by them. A mediaeval church stands near the farm, and the view over the lake is charming.

The full title of Henriette's book is *Recollections from Home* (*Erindringer fra Hjemmet*). I have only translated such passages as refer to her Uncle Søren or to his nearest relations, for example his brother Peter, Rector of Pedesborg and later Bishop of Aalborg (1805–88), known to Henriette as 'Uncle Peter'.

EXTRACTS

FROM 'RECOLLECTIONS FROM HOME' BY HENRIETTE LUND

Page 16: Henriette speaks first of her parents.

Father and mother's[1] first home! What lovely memories these words awaken! This home was not in the narrow and constricted town. My parents were enterprising rather in advance of their times, for they took up their residence just by the Lakes.[2] They lived in a beautiful house, newly erected and surrounded by gardens, just beyond the small avenues outside the North Gate. Not a stone now remains of the house; and the very place is hard to find in the large complex of new streets and buildings.[3]

It suited father and mother to live in a lonely spot outside the town. Both loved the countryside, both had a certain leaning towards romance, and both had been brought up in a quiet and responsible fashion.... Mother had known the partings which the changes and chances of life bring within a family. Her elder sister Nicoline had been married a few years before, to father's brother Christian. She then had three brothers living, of whom the only one still[4] alive, was the eldest, Peter Kierkegaard, till recently bishop of Aalborg. Then came Niels,[5] who died as a young man in America. And last, Søren Kierkegaard the author, later so well known. At that time he was little more than a boy.[6] He was of slender and delicate appearance, and ran about in a little coat of red-cabbage colour. He used to be called 'fork' by his father, because of his tendency, developed quite early, towards satirical remarks.

Although a serious, almost austere tone pervaded the Kierkegaards' house, I have the firm impression that there was a place for youthful vivacity too, even though of a more sedate and home-made kind than one is used to nowadays. And I am told that the house

[1] Ferdinand Lund and Petrea Kierkegaard.
[2] See Part I (Brøchner's *Recollections*), p. 35, note 3.
[3] Nowadays the place is as busy as any, and right in the city!
[4] i.e. in 1876 when Henriette is writing.
[5] Born 30 April 1809. He had gone to America to seek business. He had previously been in business in Copenhagen with Christian Agerskov, but was dissatisfied. After a short stay in America he died. There is touching correspondence preserved about his death from an Episcopal clergyman named Ralph Willeston. See Carl Weltzer, *Peter & Søren Kierkegaard*, pp. 47 ff.
[6] He was fifteen when Petrea married, and about sixteen years older than Henriette.

was open for a certain old-fashioned hospitality. Of the young men who visited Uncle Peter, most were budding theologians. The Kierkegaards consorted much with the Boesens. Grandfather's acquaintance with Councillor Boesen,[1] who was father of a large family of daughters and sons (many of whom were of the same age as the Kierkegaard children) was due to the Moravian brotherhood in Stormgade, of which both men were members.[2] . . . The Boesens long outlived the dissolution of the Kierkegaardian house, and I have visited them for many years. . . .

When I come to think of the life that went on in grandfather Kierkegaard's house, I feel myself so transported back on the stream of time, that not even the most distant sound from the hurry of today, with all its railway rush, reaches those days. Hurry was unknown in that house. They behaved with equanimity; and there is some justification for Uncle Søren's jesting remark, that in his home they bought the fine bread[3] a fortnight before the party! It is even said, by way of illustrating the even-tenored foresight pervading the household, that the clothes for the next child's confirmation were bought and cut while the first was going to the priest.[4]

It was held to be in due order—which appealed to grandfather—that the sons of a house so far as possible should take up different professions, and that not all should choose for example the life of a student. One son had to go into business, another had to go to sea, a third to banking, and so on. And once grandfather had taken up a notion, he was the sort of person who would see it put into practice. Since therefore Uncle Peter had entered the University, Uncle Niels ought (and so was made) to go into business, although his whole mind was set on books. This was a constant source of sorrow to him, a sorrow which overshadowed all his short life; for he never could feel himself in his right niche.

Daughters were not the most favoured creatures in such an old-time-home. Grandfather's view was that girls did not need much education. On the contrary, they must accustom themselves from early days to wait upon their more well-read brothers, and give a hand in the house. Fortunately both girls (Nicoline and Petrea), were so well-gifted, and equipped with so much natural charm, that

[1] Johannes Boesen, secretary to the treasury, married to Sophie Hammerick. His son Emil was Søren Kierkegaard's closest friend. See pp. 97, 104, 124, 133.

[2] The centre of the Moravian brotherhood was at Herrenhut, and in 1793 they got permission to build a prayer-room in Stormgade. Curiously enough the Anglican congregation, before the present Anglican Church of St. Alban's was built, worshipped in this room. See Jarvis, *History of the English Episcopal Church in Denmark*, p. 45 f.

[3] i.e. wheaten bread (perhaps the term may include cakes), as opposed to the rye bread also eaten in Denmark.

[4] i.e. for confirmation classes. In the Danish Church the priest, not the bishop, confirms.

any possible deficiencies in respect of ordinary intelligence were certainly not noticeable. But it must have been a great change for mother, with father at her side, to become mistress of her own house. For housekeeping did not at all fit in with her own gentle and somewhat brooding disposition. When in later life, with her inquiring and eager mind, she sometimes deplored the gaps she felt in her literary education, father would always answer that he was glad she had not learnt all she would have liked, since she might have looked down on him! . . .[1]

Grandfather and grandmother Kierkegaard had had two other children besides the two above named.[2] The eldest, a daughter, died when grown up; from what cause I cannot remember having ever heard.[3] The younger was a half grown boy, who died from a blow on the head which he got playing at school. Only Uncle Peter and Uncle Søren, out of all the seven children, survived their father. Grandmother too died during the years which, with so short intervals between, took off the daughters and Uncle Niels.[4] I do not remember Grandmother Kierkegaard at all, but she was said in the family to have been a nice little woman with a homely and cheerful disposition. Her sons developed intellectually far over her head.[5] Their high soaring seemed to her sorrowful heart like a soaring away from the station where she felt at home, and where she so fain would have kept them. She was therefore never so happy as when some passing indisposition forced them back under her rule. She was specially gratified when she could get them to stay in bed, because then she wielded the sceptre with joy, and looked after them and protected them like a hen protecting her chickens. Her grandchildren too profited by her motherly disposition. It often happened that if her little chubby figure did but show itself in the nursery doorway, the crying would cease, and the rebel little boy or girl would soon be asleep in her soft embrace. . . .

Grandfather outlived all his family deaths by at least four years.[6]

[1] Since Henriette was only five when her mother died, she must have got all this information from her father. She was forty-six when *he* died!

[2] There were in fact seven children in all (i) Maren Christine, 1798–1822. Of her we know almost nothing. (ii) Nicoline, 1799–1832; (iii) Petrea, 1801–34; (iv) Peter, 1805–88; (v) Søren Michael, 1807–19, died from a blow on the head; (vi) Niels Andreas, 1809–33, died in Paterson, U.S.A.; (vii) Søren Aabye, 1813–55. See *E.P.*, I, p. xxxix.

[3] i.e. Maren, mentioned above. She was twenty-four when she died.

[4] The deaths here referred to occurred as follows:— (i) Nicoline, 10 Sept. 1832, (ii) Niels, 21 Sept. 1833, (iii) the mother, M. P. Kierkegaard's second wife, 31 July 1834, (iv) Petrea, 29 Dec. 1834. Previous deaths were (i) M. P. Kierkegaard's first wife, 27 March 1796, (ii) Søren Michael, 14 Sept. 1819, (iii) Maren, 15 March 1822.

[5] Apparently she could not write, because her signature on official documents is with guided pen. Perhaps she could read a little because her eldest son tells us twice that he gave her books. See Sejer Kuhle, *S. K. i Barndom og Ungdom*, p. 21 f.

[6] He died 9 Aug. 1838.

And we his grandchildren, especially after we had moved to father's house in Gammel Torv, used to visit him often. He lived in his old house in Nytorv, between the apothecary's and the Town Hall. A tablet was later let into the wall in memory of Uncle Søren.[1]

I vividly remember grandfather's honourable figure in his long, drab-coloured coat, with his knickerbockers tucked into his top boots, a heavy stick with gold knob in his hand, and (what was not the least interesting feature to us children) pockets full of peppermints. He was of powerful build, with firm and resolute features. His head was slightly bowed, but his eyes had a distant expression, as if they were gazing out over the Jutland heath, where as a boy he had tended his sheep. Yet I think his gaze went further. . . . In his old age he longed for eternity, and his latter days were like a pilgrim's wandering in a strange land. I do not for a moment mean that his personality was sad or sickly. His speech was too vivacious and clear for that, and his gait too vigorous. He surprised people who did not know his mind, by the serenity he displayed in sorrow. For he had accustomed himself to view life's sorrows and pains with other than mere worldly eyes. Yet at the same time he was ready to help by word or deed wherever he could.

When he lost his two beloved daughters one after the other, he bowed his old grey head still lower, but also he put his hands together and thanked God who both gives and takes. And when flames surrounded his house,[2] and he was suddenly and unexpectedly faced with *that* spectacle, he put his worldly state in God's hands with the same serenity. With an almost solemn dauntlessness, he preceeded to put in order what could be ordered.

On the other hand he sometimes let himself be upset by small tribulations, and then his natural broodiness of mind was revealed. Broodiness was indeed his daily cross. He could I think, more than most people, verify Goethe's words, 'We all suffer with life.' But, unlike Goethe—that great figure in the world of art—he had taken hold upon the faith which can comfort, and which can also invest even the meanest person with a greatness of far higher importance than the wealthiest earthly life, temporally understood, can attain.

Grandfather had retired from business in his fortieth year; and from that time on his life was occupied with philosophic reading. The German philosopher Wolff was the special object of his study. And since in all he did he was thorough, penetrating, and accurate—even to painfulness—we may be sure that his reading was not frittered

[1] The house has now vanished, and an ugly bank takes its place.
[2] The house in Nytorv caught fire in Søren Kierkegaard's boyhood.

away into superficialities. How he managed to amass what was for those days a considerable fortune, seeing he was a poor boy who came to Copenhagen with nothing, would be incomprehensible to me, were I not pretty closely acquainted with the matter. I could not credit him with money-making talent; and his uprightness was almost *too* anxious and conscientious. Orderliness and frugality, even though the latter bordered upon harshness, are not sufficient to explain his success. He must also have met with some good luck and specially good luck too. And so he did. It came in a form which spelt bad luck and ruin for most other people; I refer to the Ordinance of January 1813, which, while with one blow it made many a rich man into a beggar, swelled grandfather's possessions, both in money and paper, into incredible proportions.[1] 'Royal bonds' were the only shares which escaped; and grandfather was one of the lucky people who possessed them. Far from losing his little fortune, it grew in like proportion as everything around him fell; and a steadily rising market completed the work. All one had to do at the time was to sit tight and hold on to what one had, and the fortune grew of itself.

When we children from both Købmagergade and Gammel Torv[2] spent an evening with grandfather, there was always great pomp and excitement. A long well furnished table in the old style awaited us. After the meal there were both games and playing. I do not mean instrumental playing, but Black Peter[3] and Eleven and a half.[4] True there were many table delicacies which passed by my brother and me. We were sent off with a strong injunction not to touch sour or fat things, which of course looked specially interesting. Miss Møller, grandfather's stiff yet extremely good-natured housekeeper, would thereupon shake her head provokingly with the remark, 'There are always so many things the children from Gammel Torv must not do.' But grandfather merely obeyed orders. There was to be no milk-sop sentimentality! Obedience was for him not merely *a* main prop, I think it was *the* main prop of his life. Could he lift his grey head from the earth and see the present race of men once more, he would I think use Pascal's sad words against it, and sorrowfully cry, 'The reason it is so difficult to believe is because it is so difficult to obey.'

[1] A few months before Søren Kierkegaard's birth in 1813, the Government, who had in the previous years of war issued banknotes in preposterous quantities, took the bold step of writing them down to about 1/10th of their value. This drew down all other securities, bonds and shares, except the 'royal bonds'—in deference to foreign creditors.

[2] i.e. the children of 'Uncle' Christian Lund, and Henriette's family respectively.

[3] A card game in which every card could be paired except one, 'Black Peter'. The person possessing this at the end had lost.

[4] A kind of 'Pontoon'.

Uncle Peter hardly ever came to these feasts. But Uncle Søren always came, anyway towards the close of the evening. Indeed it is from that time that my recollection of him really begins. I can even fix in my mind a precise moment when my recollection began. It was when I saw him come in at the door, take his hat from his blond hair, and pleasantly bow to us. And here I cannot refrain from one little remark. Younger people, who can only recall his appearance from the drawings in the *Corsair*,[1] or at most from having seen him in his latter days, before he succumbed to a wasting sickness—if *these* think of him almost as a caricature, it is not to be wondered at. But I remember how surprised I was a few years ago, to trace a similar, though not so extreme a misconception, in an otherwise specially beautiful article, which at that time was generally attributed to Professor Brøchner.[2]

How can one ironically exclaim, 'He certainly did not have many physical advantages,' if one has not even spoken to him once at close quarters, or seen his intelligent face and his fine figure? . . .

In the pencil sketch I have of him, his nose has a slight but refined and aristocratic curve, reminding me of a portrait of Bulwer Lytton when he was young; only Uncle Søren's nose, though curved, was more bold and fleshy. But his mouth and eyes, the shape of his head, and the mass of his hair, are excellently portrayed in my sketch. The pose also is very characteristic. His mouth was certainly large; but on the other hand, what a complete gamut of different moods found expression in its curves and lines, from gentle sorrow and tenderness to bold defiance or subtle irony—the last being not the least predominant trait! And then the eyes, they did not deteriorate with the years. Rather their natural soulful expression acquired such a heightened lustre, that they shone like stars when I saw him for the last time in hospital.

Page 25

A pleasure which I remember from grandfather Kierkegaard's house was to see them ride the Diet in. Since grandfather lived by the side of the Diet house and Law courts, it was almost as though the whole pageantry was staged for us. We stood by the window and saw the two heralds in their velvet capes upon magnificent horses in the middle of the square, while all the glittering life guards formed round in an outer half circle. The proclamation the herald read out adumbrated our pleasure for the next day, when from our own window (in Gammel Torv nearby) we could see the king in his

[1] See Brøchner, extract 22, note 6.
[2] Henriette refers to the Obituary Article of 1 Dec. 1855. See pp. 6 and 43 above.

golden coach, and all the official procession with him, ride up to open the High Courts.

Grandfather was eighty-four years old, and still so hearty that nothing suggested that his departure was imminent. Nevertheless the doctor thought it unwise for grandfather to continue his usual custom any longer of taking an emetic once a year. But grandfather liked old customs and would not let himself be advised. It appeared, however, that the doctor was right, for a few days afterwards, from the strain which the emetic induced, the old man died quietly and peacefully.[1] Uncle Søren bought the family residence after his father's death and for many years occupied part of the old dwelling while uncle Peter, at least for long periods at a time, used the other wing. Peter lived there during the lifetime of his first wife, Marie Boisen, daughter of Bishop Boisen of Lolland; and also during the first years of his marriage with Henriette Glahn, a daughter of the priest of the garrison church. Indeed he was there till he was called to the little parish of Pedersborg with Kindertofte, near Søro, when he moved for ever from Copenhagen.

Page 39: How Søren Kierkegaard's sister Petrea met Henriette's father.

How uncle Christian made acquaintance with aunt Nicoline, I am not certain I ever heard. For father, the way was in that respect open. He not only saw mother with her family round about the town; but since uncle Christian for a few years in succession spent the summer months at 'Hammershøj' near Lersøen, where mother for long periods at a time visited them, and since father had hired rooms for himself in the same place, the two frequently met each other. Father has told me how the owner of 'Hammershøj' (who really had another name, but was always called 'Hammershøj' after the place), once cried, after seeing father and mother talking together, roguishly shaking his finger the while at father, 'I know who it is to be. It is none of all those ladies you so sedulously ride with!'

Page 51

Since mother and her brothers and sisters were of the same sort of age as the Agerskov children[2] they had, I suppose, associated together to some extent. But it was specially uncle Søren, who visited

[1] Peter Kierkegaard, however, describing the scene, says that the doctor himself gave the old man the emetic. See Carl Weltzer, *Peter & Søren Kierkegaard*, p. 126.

[2] Cicelie Agerskov was a nurse maid who lived *en famille* with the Henrik Lunds. She was a relation of Michael Pedersen's first wife, Kirstine Røyen. (See pp. 56, 64).

the Agerskovs regularly as a boy. It was during a stay there, when the Agerskovs were living at Buddinge Mark, that he fell from a tree, and got such a blow in the back, that he himself, at any rate, attached importance to it as affecting the whole of his later state of health, indeed, the whole of his life. It was, he thought, the first link, perhaps, in the chains of suffering which were to lead him on his lonely way. He once told me how the aged Madame Agerskov had overawed him at the time, when, in her sedate way, being deeply distressed, she said, 'Dear child, may you sometime in your life give me as deep a joy as today you have given me sorrow!'

Mother, who was then a young wife,[1] was present at the incident, but had to drive away from the pale suffering boy, whose tears ran slowly but incessantly down his cheeks, as from an inexhaustible spring. She pressed a little purse into his hand as balm for the wound. Instant and practical help from a doctor would have certainly been better instead. Yet—nobody thought of that then.

Page 79: Henriette's stepmother's engagement to her father.

Grandfather Kierkegaard had great esteem for her (i.e. Henriette's stepmother), and he gave her away at her wedding, which took place very quietly at Pastor Waage's house. Waage was later the Rector (i.e. the head) of Søro Academy, but at the time of the wedding he was a priest of Our Lady's Church. . . . My own mother (Petrea Kierkegaard) was married by Mynster quietly at Grandfather Kierkegaard's home.

Page 81: Cicilie Agerskov's[2] house in Lyngby, where in the later years of their life, Cicilie's parents had set up a washing and bleaching establishment.

It was on an extensive plot, where gardens and meadows stretched down to the stream by Sorgenfri Wood. While the side wings of the building—extensive like the grounds, and still today called 'The Bleachery'—were let out, the old folks themselves that year occupied the main block, with its quite numerous rooms, including a spacious, old-time room opening on to a large garden which stretched

[1] Was she? She, Petrea, was married 28 Oct. 1828, and S.K. was then nearly fifteen and a half years old and already confirmed (20 April 1828). Or was the incident earlier, and Petrea still a spinster?

[2] See extract 3, with note. Lyngby is seven and a half miles from Copenhagen.

[3] Søren Kierkegaard's eldest sister Nicoline married (1824) a clothier named Johan Christian Lund. His favourite sister Petrea married Johan Christian Lund's brother, Henrik Ferdinand Lund, assistant in the National Bank. Henriette was born of this latter marriage.

down towards the bleaching ground. Since there was so much room indoors, the Agerskovs had taken in Uncle Christian's children as paying guests, i.e. my girl-cousins and the 'big boy cousins' as we called them. With them was also their housekeeper Miss Dencker. Some of the rooms in the side wings were let out to Uncle Søren, who lived there one or two years during the summer months. One fine day, when I too was sent thither and given permission to stay for some time,[1] I found there a large company, and not a little enjoyment. The company ran wild in the beautiful wood, played in the patches of field between the outstretched bleaching linen, built forts by the stream with ships to sail on it, and were lost in observing the hidden life which moved about in the stream, where sticklebacks, water beetles, and all sorts of other things, came out for a moment from their hidden quarters, only to vanish again without a trace. Uncle Søren, whom otherwise I rarely saw, took a keen interest in us that holiday, even though, as far as I was concerned anyway, it often ended in teasing. Indeed at first I was inclined to think 'Now there will be no more peace'. But I had only to set eyes on the slender figure, and hear his short, half-suppressed laughter which seemed to shake his whole person, and it was not long before I perceived an affection and tenderness concealed behind that teasing figure; and my confidence and joy at seeing him returned again. The smarter the repartee, the more uncle Søren enjoyed himself; and his little chuckling laughter became positively infectious. For lack of a felicitous rejoinder, I was once, in the heat of battle, reduced to extremes; and was so quick-handed as to give him a box on the ears. Uncle Søren could very well have said what the man did who was spat upon in Court by his opponent, 'Yes, but that proves nothing.' For a moment it looked as though a still smarter sally was hovering over my head. But my obvious confusion probably put him in a different frame of mind; for a good-natured, irresistible burst of laughter cleared up the incident. He could not for long be angry with his 'spectacled-dame' as he usually called me, making fun of my tendency to sit and stare in front of me with far-away gaze, while the whole of the outer world was lost to me—a tendency by the way which he himself had to a still greater degree! . . .

Many years afterwards, in the summer of 1856, I was visiting my brother Vilhelm's[2] parents-in-law in Ordrup. Towards evening as we approached Lyngby . . . all those far off happy summer days

[1] She was not yet ten years old. See p, 58. S.K. was not yet 26.
[2] Eldest brother of Henriette. Owner of the large farm called Annisegaard, some thirty miles from Copenhagen, where later Henriette wrote these *Recollections*. See p. 47.

came vividly to my mind. The evening bells[1] rang as of old, and the birds—yes,

> 'all the songsters good,
> that dwell in Lyngby wood'

were silent, while the sun sent his evening glance over the quiet, dreaming meadow. But where were now all the merry voices of children, which of old filled the air with their shouts of freedom? The old garden stood so empty and sad, as if it could grieve and weep with me. One voice of the many from those days, was gone for ever; one faithful lover of the gentle peaceful countryside no summer would bring back again. His sadness, his short, teasing laughter, and his great, if repressed tenderness—that was only a memory, like so much else we knew and loved. All things gradually fade away; and the heart must learn, as the poet says, 'di memoria nudrirsi piu che di spere'.

Page 102

I went to school again when I was getting on for ten years old, in spite of mother's antipathy towards girls' schools. For Uncle Søren, who usually was adamant against interfering in any way with my parents' plans, threw all his influence into the scale, because I seemed to him too introspective to endure the more isolated life which being taught at home entails. Whether it was to celebrate the happy result of his representations in this connexion, I do not know; but he invited me shortly afterwards to drive out to Lyngby with him. I remember that the tour was favoured by a lovely autumn day, and that my girl-cousin and the 'big boy cousins' were with us. Our outward journey was completed with much jollity, in which many stories were brought forward, always on the theme of school, and my future going to school. I heard with consternation various examples of how severe things could be, and this feeling did not decrease in face of the well-arranged concluding tableau which Uncle Søren was a master at. According to it, my name had been put up for fourteen days in succession upon the blackboard, so that people could get used to it before the person herself should be on view!

But though he thus mercilessly teased us, he was just as affectionately by our sides, just as carefully did he look after us. He wrapped me in his large travelling cloak on our homeward journey, which took place in deep silence. Uncle soon sank deep into reverie; while we children gradually nodded through sleepiness, or else were occupied in watching the sky and its ever-changing face.

[1] Bells are rung in church towers in Denmark at 8 a.m. and sunset. The latter always end with the Angelus.

Page 105

In the late summer of 1838, grandfather Kierkegaard died. I remember very clearly that we were visiting Uncle Christian one day while grandfather was ill, and that Uncle Søren (who arrived just as we did) took the whole thing very lightly and regarded it as a bagatelle. How heavily he took his father's death, and what sorrow the loss brought him, only became clear to me later. Perhaps indeed a certain repentance was mingled with his sorrow, over and above what we always must feel when we lose our dear ones. For we are ever in their debt, and nowhere perhaps are we reminded more painfully of all the inadequacy of our weak human nature than when we part from our parents. . . .

But for Uncle Søren, there was this very special feature, that he had not fulfilled his father's long-cherished wish to see him take a degree, 'Father thinks that a veritable Canaan lies on the other side of a theological degree, but climbs up hard by, and declares that I shall never arrive there'—so he wrote in 1835 in a letter to Uncle Vilhelm in Brazil.[1] His predominant tendency to desultory reading and (as it seemed) lack of application must really have been a very painful phenomenon for grandfather. Only later, when Uncle blossomed forth as an author, could it be seen that these years were by no means wasted. The memory of his father's grief has, however, been a sore burden for Uncle Søren's brooding nature, a burden which perhaps, like a shadow, has grown with distance. But the fact that death so suddenly took off that strong old man was bound to affect uncle's feelings all the more deeply. Nevertheless he ostensibly continued his old manner of life. He frequented coffee houses as usual, and went for walks just as eagerly in the streets. But from 7 to 11 p.m. every evening he refused visitors. In those hours he studied diligently; and in a very short time he was ready for the examination which grandfather had desired with so much longing.

Page 109: Speaking of family gatherings with Uncle Christian (husband of Nicoline Kierkegaard, and for forty-three years a widower) whose house was at the corner of Købmagergade and Klædeboderne.

Uncle Peter Kierkegaard was sometimes present at these festivities, but Uncle Søren only paid short visits, always at the same hour that he was generally accustomed to look in on Uncle Christian. He would chat a little with each person, but also liked to look at both

[1] *Journals*, 16 (I, A, 72). See p. 47.

Aunt Jens Lund and Marie Falbe, who, each in their own way, were so lovely that you rarely saw their like. . . .

After the children had grown up, parties were not lacking whenever they wanted. I remember my first children's dance, and how embarrassed I felt at this my first acquaintance with the little ladies of Copenhagen. In spite of short skirts and plaits down their backs, they had not a little of the ballroom lady about them. The young gentlemen, friends of our boy-cousins, were at first more inclined to fence with Uncle Søren and enjoy themselves with him, their avowed favourite, than to be lured by the pleasures of the dance.

Page 111

Shortly after I had started going to school, we were surprised to get the news that Uncle Søren was engaged. Soon I had to go and visit my 'new aunt' for the first time,[1] in Uncle Christian's house. She was an attractive young girl of eighteen, affectionate to a degree towards us children, and eager to win our love in return, and that was not difficult in such circumstances. Not long afterwards we were invited to her home, where everybody, and not least Uncle Søren, did their utmost to make us feel happy.

Her parents lived in one of the old buildings in Børsgade, whose back premises looked out on the present Slotsholmsgade. For me, who up till then had known little else of Copenhagen than the way from Gammel Torv to Købmagergade (the school I went to was in Købmagergade just opposite Uncle Christian's), it was now wonderful to go frequently by the arcades of the Palace and the beautiful Exchange buildings.

From her father's windows I remember having seen the procession when Princess Mariane arrived as the bride of our Prince (Frederick). A more beautifully arrayed reception can hardly be imagined. . . . There was a great company, mostly ladies, assembled at the house of 'Regina's'[2] parents. They all asked eagerly after her fiancé. But he, to their great surprise, had that very day gone off to the woods with her father. Uncle was not, you see, the only queer one!

In the course of the summer, I was allowed to go into the town from Vesterbro or Bakkehus (where I think we must have been living at the time)[3] to visit Regina. She was as affectionate as ever, but I could not help feeling that there was a cloud over the horizon, where

[1] In Sept. 1840, Søren Kierkegaard became engaged to Regine Olsen, daughter of Councillor Olsen, manager of the Finance Ministry's Chief Office.

[2] Regine was commonly called Regina by her family, and by S.K., who speaks of 'mit Hjerts herskende Regina'—queen of my heart, Regina.

[3] The Lunds had spent the summer at one or other of these places.

before all had been so bright. When we parted, she accompanied me through the courtyard leading to Slotsholmsgade, where there was a canal, at that time not filled up. I recall how surprised I was when we emerged from the shade of the courtyard into the bright sea of light, where the sun played upon the water and all the handsome buildings round about. Here we said goodbye to each other for the last time, and as I went away I saw her in the bright sunlight, with her hand over her eyes, standing in the same spot, in order to wave me a last farewell. How decidedly it was to be 'the last', we did not know then. Yet I went home with a feeling that there was something sad hanging over us.

I could not give this forboding a definite form, nor did I hear the least thing later. One day in the autumn there came an invitation, shortly after we had moved back from our summer residence into the town, to visit Uncle Søren at the old house in Nytorv where he was living with Uncle Peter, who had recently been married to Henriette Glahn. I did not know then that Uncle Søren had broken off the engagement.

Uncle Peter's first wife Marie Boisen[1] I can only remember quite dimly. I do not recall her as being beautiful, but I have a wonderfully warm impression of something very vital and cordial about her. She sang beautifully. I remember hearing her sing Bürger's 'Leonore' one evening, when my parents and I were visiting them, and everybody was very taken by her voice. Aunt Henriette on the contrary was really beautiful. She had something delicate and refined, almost noble, about her appearance, with an attractive feminine gentleness of nature. Her speech was soft, but full of grace, and she was a gracious hostess.

When we children from Gammel Torv and Kobmagergade,[2] who had received Uncle Søren's invitation, arrived at Nytorv, Aunt Henriette received us with great friendliness, happy that we (as she thought) had thought of visiting her in this way. But she was soon disillusioned when Uncle Søren arrived almost at the same moment to take us to his room. He looked terribly upset; and instead of his usual teasing, he kissed me so gently on my hair, that I was quite touched to the heart. A moment afterwards, when he was waiting to talk to us, he burst instead into violent weeping, and, without really knowing what there was to weep over—at least that was so in my case—we were soon all sobbing with him, gripped by his grief, as though under the weight of a deep sorrow.

[1] Who died childless after about one and a half years' married life.

[2] i.e. the cousins, children of the two Lunds who had married the two Miss Kierkegaards.

But uncle soon pulled himself together, and told us that one of these days he was going to Berlin, and perhaps would be away rather a long time. We must therefore promise to write to him diligently, since he would long to know how each of us was. With many tears we gave him our promise.[1]

In the drawing room, to which we shortly afterwards went, we found Uncle Peter busy reading aloud to his wife. But 'lottery' or some other game was soon brought out in our honour, and everything was done to divert us again. This however took a long time; and when Uncle Søren opened the door to ask some question or other, I remember that it went to my heart lest he should think we had now ceased to think of him. *He* looked as though he had been weeping ever since we had left him. I was in my twelfth year at the time (anno 1841) and quite unaccustomed to long handwriting. Nevertheless I kept my promise inviolate, and received answers just as regularly.

Page 115: Speaking of her childlike enthusiasm for Orla Lehmann and the new liberal movement, and of her parents' strict refusal to have this even mentioned.

After I had for some time gone quietly about with my new passion, and had found that I could not cool it by consuming Orla Lehmann's barley-sugars in great quantities, as my school friends did, I hit upon the idea one day of confiding in Uncle Søren. Bad luck *would* have it that mother should on this occasion read my effusion; and all she said, quite dryly, was 'I would advise you to re-write that letter; Uncle Søren is not interested in that subject'. And since such 'advice' was, in my experience, tantamount to a command, I was obliged to write another letter. . . .

Page 116

It was I think soon after Uncle Søren's return from Berlin that I remember another very different evening which we children spent with him. He had however by that time left his old rooms in Nytorv, for I recall that it was in his lodgings in Nørregade that we had arranged to meet. We were received in a rather ceremonious manner by our host, while Emil Boisen, later Dean of Aarhus, who was visiting Uncle, was hastily hurrying away so as not to disturb our arrangements. On our entrance, Uncle Søren made my girl-cousin and me presents of bouquets of lilies of the valley, which

[1] Søren Kierkegaard did in fact leave for Berlin, 25 Oct. 1841, fourteen days after the final breach with Regina (11 Oct. 1841).

at that time of the year[1] were rather a rarity. Then he gave each of us lovely presents. We had scarcely finished admiring these various objects, before 'Anders', Uncle Søren's faithful manservant, well-known to us as the bringer of many a happy surprise at Christmas and on birthdays, announced that a carriage was waiting at the door. 'Then we must go,' cried Uncle Søren. 'Where to?' But that nobody discovered until we arrived at the different stopping places, all prearranged, where some of the sights of the town were pointed out to us. Funnily enough the only thing I remember on this tour is a seal, whose melancholy, human eyes impressed me greatly.

When we got back, we played 'lottery' about different objects, mostly books. Then followed the evening meal, which consisted of open sandwiches, a cake of marzipan with a specially magnificent, flower-bedecked covering, and champagne. Uncle Søren was our attentive and indefatigable host, and Anders an equally kind waiter.

But since children in those days were not spoiled as they are nowadays (wine for example was reserved for rare occasions; and champagne was only used even by grown-ups at great ceremonies), father and mother did not approve this entertainment, and thought that the whole arrangement was rather overdone. I heard phrases about 'spoiling children', accompanied by this and that little fling at 'that fantastic person'.

If they regarded the celebration as only a passing whim, I think they were mistaken. For me at any rate, it is as though he wanted to celebrate a definite occasion, whose meaning, though full of significance for him, was admittedly a secret to us. Not long afterwards he wrote significantly, 'It is over; my yawl is afloat. In a moment I am where my soul longs to be, where ideas foam up with elemental fury, sounding the alarm like nations in migration. I am there, where at another time there is a quietness like the profound silence of the South Sea; a quietness such that one hears oneself speak, even though the movement goes on only in one's own heart. I am there where every moment stakes one's life, every moment loses it, and wins it again.'[3] Possibly he wished to gather us together once for all, before he went further out into that lonely deep. This was a goodbye feast; and in spite of its outer vivacity and joys, he had sorrow in his heart.

We were never again invited all together to his rooms, and we never again all met in his home. We visited him individually, we saw him when he himself paid visits, chiefly at Uncle Christian's, and

[1] Søren Kierkegaard returned from Berlin on 6 March 1842.
[2] See Brøchner's *Recollections* above, 15, note 1.
[3] *Repetition*, p. 145 (III, p. 283). Published 16 Oct. 1843, but written in Berlin, Oct. 1842–March 1843.

we used to meet him in the street. He always contrived to meet us if there was anything he wished to say, or if he desired to see us. I have a vivid impression of this, especially from my school days.

Just as when we were together at Lyngby,[1] and on many previous visits too, these meetings were not always free from a little stinging. In those easy-going days, I had, among my many other delinquencies, a sad way of having 'tulip fingers'[2] in my gloves.—And, as is so often the case, in order to avoid the bother of sewing them up, I subjected myself to numerous other and far bigger inconveniences. Thus I invented a way of concealing my lack of elegance by pulling off my glove quickly, every time I shook hands; and as an excuse for this, I pleaded to myself the example of King Christian VIII, who as a rule did this out of courtesy. One day, when I pulled off my glove in front of Uncle Søren, I was unfortunate enough to show a little ink-stained finger. He immediately cried, 'My! You have now become so learned that you go about with ink-stains on your fingers, I really hardly dare talk to you any more.' And he hurriedly disappeared!

Another time I had a still worse experience, and again my discomfiture was due to negligence. To induce tidiness, we were told to keep blotting paper in our copy-books at school; but I was not alone in often forgetting this rule. I had occasion however to admire a school friend who, when she had ink-stains on her fingers, knew how to suck them off with her plump lip. I once tried to imitate her, but was so seized with aversion that all the ink which I could not bring myself to suck off unfortunately sat outside my mouth. Since mirrors in school were regarded as superfluous, it happened still more unfortunately that the ink-stains had not quite disappeared when I went home. Fate decreed that I should again meet Uncle Søren. This time he did not even vouchsafe me a word, but passed me smilingly by with a deep bow.

At other times, however, all was sheer joy and harmony between us. He enjoyed introducing 'his little niece' to people he liked. 'There goes Professor Sibbern. Come, you must get a little closer view of the man'—and so on.

The streets of Copenhagen were in fact a large reception room for him, where he wandered early and late, and talked to everybody he wanted to. When he had left us, and I was to meet his well-known and loving figure no more, it seemed to me as if the whole town had suddenly become empty and strange. For of course by that time I took longer walks than to and from school.[3] And how

[1] See p. 56f.
[2] i.e. the fingers were worn or torn and fell back like tulip petals going over.
[3] Henriette was twenty-six when S.K. died.

often had the arcades of the Palace on Sunday mornings, or the many sudden turnings in the side streets of our neighbourhood which the afternoon sun in early spring lit up with a fleeting smile, or the ramparts on fresh winter mornings, brought me a greeting and a conversation with him whom I now missed!

I still remember one little incident from my school days, when Uncle Søren's faithful Anders had to play a trick on me. It was I think on my twelfth birthday. Anders brought me in the early morning a letter from Uncle Søren which contained only a very primitive pen sketch portraying a flower. Underneath was added in large letters 'But do not show it to anybody, for it is so shy'. This referred to the fact that, shortly before, I had presented him with a drawing, and had probably then used this truly schoolgirl expression. But my resentment at this unexpected treatment had scarcely had time to develop, before the indefatigable Anders came back with another letter with a quite different content, and accompanied by a parcel which turned out to be Paul Møller's[1] posthumous works.

Only a few days earlier at my cousins', I had got hold of a book which soon brought me into the same condition as the man of whom the Spanish king remarked, 'He must either be mad, or reading Don Quixote.' It was the story of 'Curly Fritz', which gave me a great deal of laughter and entertainment. Now that this treasure was my own lawful possession, I could scarcely find words to tell Uncle Søren how enthusiastic I felt about it. Nevertheless he felt somewhat disappointed that I had seen 'Paul Møller' before he gave it me.

After that he gave me no more books, still less sent me his own. That was against his principle. But I did get leave to borrow books freely from his library, and keep them as long as I wished.

It would seem rather as if his desire was to look after my musical education. His gifts, such as the music to *The White Lady*,[2] *Figaro*, and many other things, make me still think this. Yet he was concerned only that I should learn in all modesty to enjoy my own self through the magic sounds, and had no interest in my 'going further'. 'Simple food is the best' he used to say.

Page 145: Henriette speaks of her confirmation, and the masses of lovely flowers she received. She then continues:

When we came home from church I remember that Uncle Søren sat and waited for us. Generally speaking he visited us rarely after

[1] See Brøchner's *Recollections* above, extract 36, note 1.
[2] Opera by F. A. Boieldieu (1775–1834).

father's second marriage. He did not stay long that day either. But the next day he sent a letter (together with a present) in which he expressed his good wishes to me most intimately. Uncle Peter, who could not be present, wrote to me in similar terms.

Page 145

Some time after my confirmation, my girl cousin and I were invited to visit Pedersborg Rectory, where Uncle Peter was then priest. Together with my cousin's mother, and riding in Uncle Christian's own carriage (which he disposed of shortly afterwards, having given his horse to the army when the war of 1848 broke out)[1] we reached the friendly rectory one lovely summer evening. The rectory garden still bears clear traces of having belonged to an old castle. One could still see remains of the old ramparts surrounding the garden.

The first Saturday after our arrival, a mail coach rolled into the courtyard with a lonely passenger. It soon appeared that the lonely one was Uncle Søren. What a flutter arose in the dovecots! Sunday morning broke with cloudless skies; so the lunch table was set out in the open on one of the hillocks in the garden, and I remember still with what vivacity Uncle Søren led the conversation, and how many amusing stories he told for our benefit. But in the evening, when we settled ourselves on the grass by the little Pedersborg lake, his brilliant jollity was broken as with one stroke. In deep silence he merely gazed dreamily forward; and only when the moon, like a half-effaced death-mask, looked down on us from the faint-hued June sky, did he break the silence again, by greeting the moon in subdued and moving tones with Aladdin's words:

'O pale moon!
Thou that dividest the seasons here on earth,
Why art thou then so strait towards me, thou cold,
Thou sallow miser? Why art thou so mean? etc.[2]

The next day saw him on his homeward way again, in spite of all our entreaties. He would never allow himself a long holiday.

Page 150

Henriette next describes a visit paid to Pedersborg by the great novelist and poet B. J. Ingemann (1789–1862) who from 1822 onwards was for many years a teacher in the neighbouring public school for boys at Sorø. A merry party ensued, and Henriette looks back on it as the last jollity she had in her somewhat dry, empty and sad life. She attributes this barrenness partly to lack of

[1] See Brøchner's *Recollections*, page 25, note 3. [2] Oehlenschläger's *Aladdin*.

occupation, and partly to the family tendency to broodiness. Uncle Søren evidently detected what was wrong.

Once in the last years of Uncle Søren's life, when I met him in the street, he spoke with enthusiasm about ladies' needlework. He thought such occupation was enviable because of the rest it inevitably must bring. But rest, if it is to be healthy and natural, presupposes work. You cannot begin with it, nor does it find place in an already monotonous existence.

She goes on to say that needlework became her Alpha and Omega. Her second mother, who was not so much older than she, did find rest in needlework. She did not see that Henriette had powers which ought to have been put to use. Henriette longed, for example, after learning, but the customs of the time and her mother's will denied it to her. She envied people of less earthly fortune, who had access to learning, while she, secure and well-placed temporally, was denied it.

Even if I had turned to Uncle Søren (who with his sharpsightedness had seen my longing, and had done what he could to get me to school), I should have got no other response than his favourite retort 'Simple food is best'. Had he seen me upset and worried, he would only have thought all interference untimely, and feared to retard any progress towards eternity and 'the one thing needful'[1] which might be stirring in me. And truly, what is human sympathy with its petty resources and shortsighted calculations, compared with God's mercy which desires something more than our mere temporal weal? Those seemingly so unfruitful . . . and barren years had, I am now convinced, their purpose. My self-will was somewhat curbed, and my youthful pride broken.[2]

Page 151

The pet aversion of the century, Byron, became my fondest reading . . . Uncle Søren's books also were my very dear company. After his pseudonymous books came his religious writings,[3] and

[1] The theme of *Purity of Heart* is that this means 'to will one thing'.

[2] If Henriette had asked Uncle Søren's advice, and he had taken the line she here indicates, he would have been very wrong; not in preventing her seeking the eternal and 'the one thing needful', but in thinking this incompatible with Henriette's education. But the trend of Søren Kierkegaard's thought shows that he would not have accepted this opposition, though I fear he was the son of his age in not seeing the importance of women's education.

[3] The first series of S. Kierkegaard's books he calls 'aesthetic', and they are pseudonymous; presenting Christianity obliquely. After 1846 he largely gave up pseudonymity, and wrote directly Christian works.

unlike so many people, I did not find them heavy or intensely demanding. In those days I went about (to quote a friend's words), as in a perpetual tragedy, and I drank in his gentle comforting phrases with eagerness. . . . The 'next day'[1] existed no more for my brooding fantasy.

Henriette speaks of how her father often got monitions, as from another world, about his departed loved ones.

Father also thought he had a monition of Uncle Søren's death. He heard a plaintive sigh from Uncle's well-known voice. He had heard it and been moved by it, the very evening—indeed at the very stroke of the clock—which, as it afterwards appeared, was uncle's last hour upon earth.

However rarely my father saw Uncle Søren, and however different were the two men in spiritual development—a fact which my father used to substantiate by telling of a painting Uncle Søren once gave him as a reward 'because he was wise enough never to read a little of his (Søren's) writing's'—it could not be otherwise that my father should hold this brother-in-law dear. For Søren was his departed wife's favourite brother, and was certainly very much like her in many ways. Uncle Søren for his part entertained warm feelings for my father. I am reminded of this by a little letter I saved from the flames on one of those sad days when I took leave of our old home in Gammel Torv, when much more was burnt and destroyed than I should have found necessary in a calmer time. The letter was from Uncle Søren for one of father's birthdays. In it, he warmly expressed his recognition of my father's worth. Father's quiet constancy in always being unchangeably the same attracted Uncle. I gave this letter later to my brother Troels.[2]

Page 167

The picture which Uncle Søren gave my father was really a present given in gratitude because my father looked after his money affairs. This however was not a difficult task: in accordance with Uncle Søren's own arrangement his fortune was quite simply divided into portions, which he used up little by little with the greatest equanimity. He did not live as a rich man; he shared quietly with many a needy person, and did nothing to insure against the future. Security of possessions, and what the world calls success, he regarded only as

[1] Kierkegaard often says that dread is 'the next day'.

[2] i.e. Henriette's youngest half-brother, the historian. He wrote an account of Søren Kierkegaard in his *Bakkehus og Solbjerg*, Vol. III. It is somewhat fanciful, but valuable nevertheless.

things which retard and burden a pilgrim to the land of eternity; and in quiet daily self-forgetfulness he sought to realize this ideal of life—truly a far different thing from the eager covetousness of most people.

And yet we all must pass through death's narrow portal. We all must experience loneliness, certainly at life's last dread hour, if not earlier. Well for us then, if we have not bound our hearts to the things we must necessarily leave behind; if we have trained ourselves to be alone with God, so that that last hour may not affright us; if we have learnt to know what that hope is which can carry us securely through our earthly needs and sorrows. Then we can say, as does the hymn which Uncle wished should be inscribed over his grave[1]:

'Tis but a little while
And I have won;
My warfare here on earth
For ever done.
In Paradise at peace
World without end,
With Jesus I'll not cease
To speak, as friend.

I well remember the day when my father came home from the bank and told us that Uncle Søren had been in to fetch his last portion. It was in the winter of '55. Father had looked worried and questioningly at him, and he had answered with a long serious look. 'Goodness knows what Søren is thinking about' added my father with a sigh.

Although Uncle Søren used to visit Uncle Christian Lund fairly regularly, yet his nature seemed strange, and his whole development inexplicable, to this brother-in-law. Many a time I have enjoyed the disputes which in all good-will took place between them, and which almost invariably ended by Uncle Søren turning his head right away from his opponent, looking out into the empty room with

[1] It is by the poet Brorson (1694–1764) and does stand, according to Kierkegaard's wish, on his gravestone. I give my own translation. Henriette does not quote the verse exactly as it stands on the grave. She writes *Da* for *Saa* in her second line, and *fryde mig* (be glad) for *hvile mig* (rest) in her third. Her last two lines but one read, *Og der evindelig, Hos Gud i Himmerig*. On the grave stands *Og uafladelig*. I fancy the gravestone version is the original, for the verse has been altered in later hymn books, and from one of them possibly Henriette quotes.

The verse which stands on the grave reads as follows:

Det er en liden Tid
Saa har jeg vundet
Saa er den ganske Strid
Med Eet forsvundet,
Saa kan jeg hvile mig
I Rosensale
Og uafladelig
Min Jesum tale.

a face which gleamed with satire and saying with emphasis on every syllable: 'That was devilish good.'

When, many years later, the first volume of his 'Posthumous Papers' was published, I remember smiling to myself when I heard Uncle Christian's remarks *à propos* them—'How very odd that a man who always looked so happy was so completely pensive! But how could anyone be in cheerful spirits who ate up his fortune as he did?' Yet, this misjudgement is a mere trifle compared with the perverse way that I have time and again heard strangers pass judgement on Uncle Søren.[1]

Before I leave the subject of how the unaccountable sometimes meets us in life, I would like to say that I am little inclined to deny its possibility in others because I think I have, to some extent, experienced it myself. But since all that belongs to a part of my life which is irrelevant here, I shall not dwell upon it.

Seeing however that what I am now saying concerns Uncle Søren, I cannot refrain from relating a dream of which he formed part, and which moved me by its tremendous vividness, even though it cannot be said to have contained anything supernatural. Why it should have made such an impression on me, I do not wish to say. I can only explain that it was at a time when I had had sorrow, and when a certain disquiet in respect of religion had seized me.

I dreamt one night that I went for my usual morning walk and that Uncle Søren, just as in the old days, suddenly came walking towards me clear as life. It is said that after ten years not even the best of memories can altogether accurately retain the image of a departed one. Uncle had now been dead for more than ten years, but not

[1] Kierkegaard used, as a student, to visit Professor Sibbern at the professor's house, and later on, Sibbern sometimes accompanied Kierkegaard when he walked the streets or took his customary carriage-drives. Sibbern seems to have had the insight to reckon up his students well, and yet he never suspected for a moment that Kierkegaard suffered from inner broodiness. Neither did Kierkegaard's headmaster, Michael Nielsen, when as a boy, and later (for a time) as teacher, he belonged to Nielsen's school. Nielsen calls him *letsindig*, i.e. wanton. And here is a letter from Sibbern, dated 19 Sept. 1869, and written when he was eighty-four years old. It is to H. P. Barfod, first editor of part of Kierkegaard's *Papirer*; and is quoted by P. A. Heiberg in *Søren Kierkegaard i Barndom og Ungdom*, p. 9. 'I have not found Kierkegaard in the least "lonesome", and would never have applied such an epithet to him. He walked abroad a great deal, visited a great deal, including in his later years the poet A. S. Ørsted, who enjoyed his company greatly, but became estranged when Kierkegaard besmirched Mynster's memory. I can honestly say that he was never heavy and broody in all the long time I have known him, and it was only in the last two or three years of his life that I ceased to see him. To be a cross-bearer, and to preach the cross, are two very different things; the latter one can do to entire satisfaction. In my house we think a lot of Kierkegaard's writings. It astonishes me that one who throughout all the time I have known him hated agitation, should himself become an eager agitator. That makes me realize that a man can carry on a deep broodiness within him alongside much vivacity.' Clearly the Mynster-attack showed Sibbern a quite different Kierkegaard from the one he had previously known. So too the later Kierkegaard seemed to many quite other than the Kierkegaard they had known personally—and misunderstood.

even life itself, and the clear light of day, could have brought him more vividly before my eyes. With a well-known movement, while still at a distance, he drew out his large white pocket-handkerchief; and when he stood facing me, with what tenderness and sympathy he looked upon me! What he said I cannot reproduce; I do not rightly know if he said anything at all. But in that ghostly manner in which such things happen in dreams, I got both a premonition that the cause of my sorrow would remain, and yet that comfort would come; to which there was added a sign which indicated that I should speak to Uncle Peter Kierkegaard.

Actually the first news which met me next morning was the information that Uncle Peter Kierkegaard was expected in Copenhagen that very afternoon from Aalborg.[1] I followed the hint I had been given in my dream, and not only then, but many times afterwards, I found comfort and peace in talking to Uncle Peter.

But back to the time when Uncle Søren was still alive. Latterly I saw far less of him than in my childhood days, when he always took care to see us children from time to time. I knew quite well that his chief reason for not seeing much of us was the fear of dragging us into the kind of publicity he suffered from on different occasions, because the great mass of the public could not understand him. To me at least, he spoke openly of this as being common knowledge. But how far I was at that time from understanding what sacrifice it cost him! I had myself yet to learn the extent of the tenderness, the almost quivering pain with which children of one's family can twine themselves round one's heart. One is not always permitted to protect them as one would choose, but even the sight of them is a joy and consolation in many a lonesome moment.

No, I certainly did not realize all this then. Nevertheless, I remember how one summer afternoon, quite contrary to his usual practice, Uncle came to see us at Gammel Bakkehus.[2] I was surprised by the accuracy with which he almost apologetically declared that he had not seen me more than three times that year. The reason why his arithmetic was so good could only have been because the figure was not what he would have wished.

That same evening stands out very clearly in my mind. It had been a warm day, and a fatiguing one to many people. It was as if Nature herself rested after the sun's burning heat; even the poplars, which generally rustle, seemed to keep silence for a time in a drowsy stillness, and all the old estate lay enveloped in a dim glimmer of

[1] Where by this time he was Bishop.
[2] This was a summer house where Henriette and her parents often stayed, near Copenhagen.

mist, while from neighbouring houses and farms people emerged to enjoy the cool air. In the nearby home of the then Minister Hall,[1] a whole circle of gentlemen were still sitting out when we went a little way with Uncle Søren on his return journey to Copenhagen. 'You promised to look in on us on your way home, Dr. Kierkegaard,' they one and all shouted after him. 'Well, I am looking as hard as I can,' was the playful answer, while he bowed and swung his thin stick in the air.

Page 171

I once met Uncle Søren in my quite early youth, and I remember that he chaffed me for not being willing to give up the right to my own opinion about something or other under discussion. A dispute followed in which I tried to show my dignity and maturity in the intellectual sphere. One argument was adduced which immediately struck him. I had exclaimed, 'Yes, because I have learnt to appreciate love.' With a changed expression, but with seriousness in his voice he answered at once, 'That is another thing. You are right; now I perceive you really are grown up!' The incident still stands out in my memory. It was as though, in an excess of politeness, he had taken off his hat and bowed to me.

Although victory was thus conceded, and by such a keen observer to boot, I feel now, with the experience of later years, that I had used the phrase quite out of the blue. My sense of reality awoke so late that I could not possibly at that time have had the spiritual maturity necessary to express myself thus; the words suggest a serious grip upon life, and this Uncle Søren must have thought I had. Strictly brought up as I was and of a rather retiring, sensitive disposition, I was (both in my own nature and in my relationships with others) inclined to be biased in favour of the intellectual. Life therefore had to get a strong hold upon me before I was able not only to acknowledge verbally but also to feel in my innermost heart that love is the spring of life; even though its roses, for most people, grow in the valleys. Much conflict had yet to be gone through before I should learn to give heed to more modest gifts than the intellect; to respect those 'homely natures' which certainly are not rare in life; to know what the mortar is which holds the stones of the building together. As yet my attitude could only be compared with the sight I have often seen from our summer-house, when the mists over distant Copenhagen melted away and its towers and large buildings appeared to the sight.

[1] This must be Carl Christian Hall (1812–88). He became Cultus Minister in 1854, so Henriette is here recalling an incident when she must have been twenty-five, and Uncle Søren forty-one—a year in fact before his death when his attacks on the Church had begun or were about to begin.

It was only the great and unusual, both in life and literature, that were then able to awake my interest.

Once in the latter years of his life, when I met Uncle Søren in the street, he expressed astonishment at the interest I had in Shakespeare's *Hamlet*, which led me to read it over and over again, both in the original[1] and in translation, and also to follow performances of it with rapt attention down to the least detail. I tried to make him participate in the matter by asking him whether he himself was not gripped by that remarkable drama; whether he was not moved in the same way. 'Yes, but for me it has a special meaning,' he replied. And when I looked questioningly at him, he added by way of explanation, 'You cannot understand that now—perhaps one day you will.'[2]

In later years, as I have recalled these words, I have felt with sadness what a sympathetic relationship there must have been at that period of his life, between him and that melancholy prince, with whom 'resolution, red as the dawn' always yielded to 'pale reflexion', and to whom the spirit from the bowels of the earth constantly called, telling him to speak and act. Such a voice—not beckoning from the depths of the earth, but from the depths of his own soul—spoke also to Uncle Søren. Listener as he had become by long and faithful practice in the service of the Idea[3] he did not mistake its meaning, but knew well what was his mission in life and understood with dread that the hardest part was still to come. For in a quite different way from Hamlet he would have to summon attention, in order to maintain the right of the Idea against an effeminate and pampered generation; to point out the danger of conventional attendance at the State church; in a word, to wake, wake all those who were slumbering and smug—and men love slumber and smugness. But after the glow of resolution, pale reflexion tempted him, as it did Hamlet. It told him that humanly speaking he would get the worst of the fight; it showed him that he, who by nature was specially endowed with an eminent skill for adroitly avoiding such a thing, would only make himself a target for all and sundry, so that weapons both clumsy and agile would be directed against him; showed him finally that he himself also would have to deal out wounds and thrusts which would hurt him deeply. But when one stands alone upon the battlefield one cannot be soft-hearted (by nature he certainly was that in no small degree). The Idea's high and pure beauty had strengthened him in his fight; and who could with more justice fight

[1] Søren Kierkegaard, alas, could not read English, and so could only read it in the German translation.

[2] Søren Kierkegaard thought of himself as resembling Hamlet, as his works constantly show.

[3] A Hegelian term meaning the totality of Truth. See p. 42, note 2.

in its light than he, who stood so completely detached from all the contemporary scene, so completely removed from all personal spite and personal interest?

But he fought at the last as one whose time is short, and who therefore must bring everything to a head forcibly. He felt the earth shake under him. No wonder therefore if mistakes and one-sidedness appear. One-sidedness; yes, that is the indictment; but we must remember that without a vigorous one-sidedness, things are seldom put right; through the narrow cleft goes the most rapid stream, and people whose call it is to dig up some treasure, some element of truth which has got lost or distorted in the maelstrom of time—they have no eye for anything else but the one thing for which, with humble trust, they sacrifice their pleasure by day, and their rest by night—yes, their heart's-blood also if that is required of them. Others then have to step in and deal with the booty, sort it out, and—find flaws in it.

In this last struggle, in that year of strain, Uncle Søren did not forget those nearest to him. I cannot say for certain whether it was he who was the first to suggest to Uncle Christian Lund and my girl-cousin the idea of making a tour abroad, having as our objectives Paris and London, whither one of my brothers and one of my boy cousins had lately gone. But Uncle Søren was glad about it, and I knew for certain that he was anxious for me to go too. The feeling that we should take the struggle he was engaged in too much to heart worried him, and so he said good-bye with a look of entire satisfaction; yes, in the very moment of farewell he got an opportunity to whisper in my ear, with a little of his old teasing manner, 'And don't forget your own mother tongue!'

At the beginning of the same autumn there suddenly came the news that Uncle Søren had fallen unconscious in the street. A carriage was fetched, and he was taken to Frederik's Hospital. I was out when the news reached me. I hastened home, and was able straight away to accompany Father, who was just about to go to see him. I cannot now remember whether it was in the hospital itself or on the way to it, that I heard that Uncle Søren had said to those who received him, much as did Tasso before him on his entrance to the Monastery of St. Honofrius, 'I have come here to die'. But that a feeling of victory was mingled with his suffering and sadness—of that I got the impression the moment I stepped into the little room[1] and was met by the gleam of light which as it were radiated from his face. Never in such a manner have I seen the spirit break through its earthly frame and lend it a radiance as if it were the glorified body

[1] We may recall that Henriette was twenty-six years old at the time, so she is speaking as a mature young woman, not as a child.

at the dawn of the resurrection day. Once afterwards, when I visited him, I got a different impression, and the painfulness of the illness was more to the fore. But that first visit, and also his loving farewell, I can never forget.[1]

When this last sad time of sickness was ended by death on 11 November 1855, I, for my part, was so taken up with past times, that the thought of what was at hand hardly crossed my mind. Whether that was the case with the others, I know not. Perhaps nobody felt a very decisive call to take matters in hand. One person was a little too inclined to lean upon another; and that I suppose is how it came about that small incidental matters were allowed to be decisive—for example in the matter of choosing the day for the funeral. That this fell on a Sunday ought to have been avoided. The great stir which *The Instant*[2] had aroused, not least in a class of society which never understood how to separate the kernel from the husk, made it still more unfortunate.

Uncle Peter Kierkegaard felt the same when he came to Copenhagen from Pedersborg and found things arranged in this way. But when many of the city clergy urged upon him the request that he as a churchman ought to alter the decision, he maintained that a change now at the last moment would only be viewed as cowardice, and therefore ought not to be entertained. So there the matter was allowed to rest.

But I remember the painful feeling which took hold of me, when that Sunday, in the Church of Our Lady,[3] from a seat in the gallery, I looked over the nave of the Church where the tightly packed mass of people heaved like a tossing sea, while a ring of quite sinister-looking

[1] Henriette evidently also visited the hospital after her Uncle's death, for speaking of a friend of hers named Augusta Essendrop, she says that they parted 'only a few months before her death, when I returned from the hospital where I had seen Uncle Søren's dear face fixed in death' (p. 95).

[2] The name given to the series of pamphlets which Søren Kierkegaard published, attacking the Church.

[3] The Cathedral Church of Copenhagen. It was founded in the twelfth century, burnt in 1728, restored and re-consecrated 1738; burnt again and destroyed by the British bombardment under Nelson 1807. It was the only considerable medieval building left in Copenhagen, where many fires had destroyed most of the old city by about 1795. Today, most of the oldest buildings date only from the seventeen and eighteenth century, though they are very beautiful indeed. All the churches in the centre of the city are, as in London, classical. So is the Church of Our Lady here referred to. At the bombardment, Mynster was the first assistant-priest there. The congregation, which was a large one (attracted by Mynster's preaching), had to migrate to Trinity Church during the rebuilding (1811–29). Hence Kierkegaard, whose father belonged to Mynster's congregation, and had Mynster as his spiritual guide, had to be baptized elsewhere (in the Church of the Holy Spirit, 3 June 1813) and was confirmed by Mynster in the Trinity Church, 28 April 1828, i.e. just before his fifteenth birthday. The present Cathedral is a heavy classical building with a square campanile which is a complete contrast to the spires of other churches. It has six Doric pillars over its portal, and two large statues (of Moses with his tables, to the right, and David to the left). Inside are the figures of the twelve Apostles by Thorvaldsen standing round the walls, and behind the altar is the figure (also by Thorvaldsen), of the Christ with outstretched arms. Underneath this figure are inscribed the words 'Come unto me'.

figures had settled itself round the flower-bedecked coffin. Then the church doors opened, and to my joy a close band of an entirely different appearance pressed in. This band wished to follow Denmark's great thinker to the grave, and stand as a guard of honour round the coffin. But could they get near enough? With entire sympathy I noticed in the forefront a powerful figure, who dauntlessly made his way through. The others followed him equally undaunted, until they had won their position and formed a ring, which, like a strong wall, replaced the other ring.

Of priests in vestments, I saw only, besides Uncle Peter Kierkegaard, old Dean Tryde. Had I been in normal spirits, I should certainly have smiled at the sight of him, for he obviously found himself ill at ease. He pushed his little skull-cap backwards and forwards on his head with a feverish haste, while his face, generally so mild, wore a very troubled expression. But now Uncle Peter stood up, and soon the skull-cap was allowed to remain in peace. The restless sea of people became still as mice, and I was able to weep in silence while Uncle Peter spoke first of the old home with its flourishing youth, a home of which he himself was now the only survivor. Then he dwelt upon the deceased, and in a well-ordered, powerful speech, tried to sketch the latter's importance for the Church.

After the coffin was borne out, and the ceremony over, I remember that the late Peter Boisen,[1] a brother to Uncle Peter's first wife, came up to me to comfort me in his gentle way. But more clearly still, I remember even now, how my mother, when I got home, came into my little room, sat down quietly, and with that dignity of which she was capable (a dignity which had something surprisingly sorrowful about it, together with a passing appearance of weakness), bade me not think so much about the dead and weep so much over them, since it could not alter things. Far better think about the living, whom we still had with us and could serve and please. True, words, and healthy thoughts, which with every new bereavement we are all too prone to forget. But there is comfort in always having a problem to face, however weakly and imperfectly we make ever new endeavours to solve it.

Page 177

A few years before Uncle Søren's illness and death, I went one Sunday to Vartov Church.[2] . . . I was so taken by the hearty hymn

[1] Peter Outzen Boisen (1815–62) son of Bishop P. O. Boisen, assistant-priest of Vartov, an enthusiastic admirer of N. F. S. Grundtvig, whose daughter, Meta Grundtvig, he married.

[2] Where Grundtvig was priest. It was, and still is, of the Pietistic type. Grundtvig is Denmark's greatest hymn-writer, as Kierkegaard confesses. Otherwise Kierkegaard criticizes him much.

singing, which in those days was something quite unusual, and also by the spirituality of the whole service, that I continued my visits, and only smiled when, on one of my first walks to the church I met Uncle Søren, who *en passant* remarked with a smile, 'It would not usually be good to come to Vartov.'

Mother liked this tendency of mine just as little. She was an eager disciple of Mynster and I need hardly depict how badly she was affected later on by Uncle Søren's attack on him, and the strife connected therewith. I however keep in thankful remembrance what I personally owe to Grundtvig and his circle of close adherents. He aroused in me an appreciation of the treasury of old church hymns, and I appreciated also all the new hymns he himself added with such bountiful hand. And I am glad to recall how this treausury also evoked a response from mother towards the end of her life. For in those sad days when she needed the comfort and solace which a sincere Christian hymn can bring, only I could make the right choice.

She died four years after Uncle Søren; and so exactly did the dates correspond, that the last day she was up and about, was precisely the day of his death, 11 November.

Part III

KIERKEGAARD'S DEATH AND LAST STRUGGLE WITH THE CHURCH

INTRODUCTION TO PART III:

THE DEATH OF KIERKEGAARD

Kierkegaard died on 11 November 1855 and was buried on 18 November in the Church of Our Lady, the Cathedral Church of Copenhagen. At the cemetery afterwards, a 'scene' was made by Henrik Lund. A nearer glimpse is here given from contemporary documents of what exactly happened at the cemetery. Henriette herself was not present, nor has Brøchner mentioned the incident.

The note to extract 50 in Brøchner's *Recollections* (page 39) mentions that Kierkegaard had attacked the Danish Church, and that at the time of his death his attack had been in full swing for some ten or eleven months. In fact he had been 'loading the gun' for it since about 1846. He had long felt dissatisfaction with the emasculated form of Christianity he considered the Danish Church was presenting. That Church was, and still is, a State Church financed by a Government tax and looked after on its material side by a Church Minister (in Kierkegaard's day called the Cultus Minister because his functions were wider) with portfolio in the Government. Kierkegaard's death was so closely connected, both chronologically, and perhaps causally, with his attack on the Church, that it is impossible to deal properly with the one without the other. Kierkegaard felt that Bishop Mynster, the Danish Primate, and also the Danish clergy, were more concerned to keep on the right side of the Government, and not jeopardize their safe jobs, than to preach Christianity 'neat'. So at long last, after much cogitation, he started a public attack. It began in the *Fatherland*, in that paper's issue of 18 December 1854. The occasion was that in a public speech Bishop Martensen, Mynster's successor, described Mynster as a true 'witness for the truth'. This description outraged Kierkegaard, and he continued his attacks with twenty articles in the *Fatherland*; interspersing these with an article, printed as a separate broadsheet, entitled *This has to be said.* (This is referred to in a Diary extract by Peter Kierkegaard, Søren's brother, see p. 117). It was accompanied by another sheet entitled *The Midnight Cry*, and the two were published in May 1855. That same month appeared Kierkegaard's last article in the *Fatherland* upbraiding Bishop Martensen for his silence. After this Kierkegaard started his own paper called *The Instant* (*Øiblikket*) which came out about every fortnight. Each issue contained about seven or eight articles, all by Kierkegaard himself. They may be read in Lowrie's translation entitled (after Geismar) *Attack on Christendom.* See also Hohlenberg's *Kierkegaard,* and my own *Kierkegaard Commentary.* Henriette Lund defends her uncle against the undoubtedly true charge (as she recognizes), of overdriving the attack (see p. 74). But though overdriven the articles are not nonsense, and they give us all, not least the clergy, food for anxious thought. (See p. 106, letter 11 below.)

Part III of this book which follows, deals both with the attack on the church and also with Kierkegaard's death.

Section I contains contemporary newspaper reports. There is inevitably some redundancy, but each gives its own slant and illuminating point of view. No. 1 is the bare announcement of Kierkegaard's death the day after it occurred. No. 2 is a short account, the day after it happened, of the funeral and the committal. Note Dean Tryde's objection to Henrik Lund's speech at the cemetery. No. 3 gives a glimpse of the interest in Kierkegaard both in Sweden and Scandinavia generally. It mentions the crucial phrase 'witness for truth'. No. 4 shows that people were wondering about the tactfulness (the word 'tactless' was bandied about a good deal in this affair), of having a church funeral at all. Nos. 3, 5, and 6, give a country paper's accounts, No. 5 mooting the question (which happily came to nothing), of founding a sect after Kierkegaard. This was the very thing he had so set himself against; though it is true that N. P. Grunnett, who founded a free-church sect, claims to have been influenced by Kierkegaard, and so too does P. C. Trandberg, who was connected with the founding of the Lutheran Mission Society,[1] (It is easy and common for the unorthodox to refer themselves to Kierkegaard!) Nos. 6 and 8 give a fairly extended account of what happened at the cemetery. No. 7 discusses, rather than relates, what happened; and this in a dignified and worthy manner.

Section II presents glimpses of reactions, both private and public, to the events we are considering. I may perhaps draw special attention to the favourable reactions of Pastors Kofoed-Hansen and Lange, and to the latter's visit to Kierkegaard's sick bed; a visit I think hitherto unnoticed by English commentators.

Section III gives ten fairly intimate letters about Kierkegaard's last sickness, mostly from members of his family, and all showing great tenderness.

Section IV is of special importance as being the recollections of Henriette's half-brother Troels Lund, then a boy of fifteen, later an historian of repute. Troels corroborates and completes what Henri-

[1] M. Neiindam: *Free Churches & Sects,* pp. 361 ff. and 374 ff.

ette says about the sick bed and the funeral, and adds intimate glimpses of the Lunds, which those wanting to understand Kierkegaard will appreciate.

Section V may have special importance because it elucidates what has seemed to many people a hard spot in Kierkegaard's make-up—his attitude to his brother Peter, and notably his refusal to see Peter on his deathbed. Peter's own words on the subject (which are here given) are helpful, and have never before been presented to the English reader.

Section VI is the moving last correspondence of Regine Schlegel (*neé* Olsen), Kierkegaard's former fiancée. The documents reveal at first hand that she retained her feelings of respect for Kierkegaard. The story of the engagement is well known. Kierkegaard felt he could not be an ideal husband, and so he caused Regine by rough behaviour to break off the engagement, though he loved her to the end. Evidently she was not deceived by his behaviour, and though she married Fritz Schlegel and went out with him to the Danish West Indies (since sold to America), where he was Governor, she never doubted his real sincerity. Now as an older woman (she was born January 1823 and so would be about thirty-three at the time of these letters), she says how sad she was not to have clarified things with Kierkegaard before he died. She appeals to Henrik Lund to say and do what he can to clear certain things up. The letters bring the whole incident to as felicitous a close as possible.

I. NEWSPAPER REPORTS

1

Yesterday evening, after being confined to bed for a short time, Denmark's greatest religious author, Dr. Søren Kierkegaard died, aged forty-three.[1] He wanted to stir up people's sense of religion, and many will assuredly remember with gratitude that he set serious thoughts going in their hearts; thoughts which, through his help, have acquired such power in their souls, that they will never more forsake them.

From the *Fatherland*, 12 November 1855

2

If witness be needed that it was an exceptional person who was yesterday committed to earth, such witness was given by the thousands who filled every inch of the Church of Our Lady. Indeed the church, except for lack of funeral decorations, looked exactly as it did at the funerals of Thorvaldsen, Oehlenschlaeger, and Ørsted.

The deceased's brother, Pastor P. C. Kierkegaard, Dr.Theol., gave a funeral oration, wherein, with intended emphasis, he repeatedly blamed and condemned his brother's point of view and recent activities. The choice of time and place seemed likewise designed as a protest against these things: at least if this were not the intention, then the whole funeral was arranged with singular tactlessness.

The committal was carried out by Dean Tryde at the Assistance Cemetery; and when the funeral was over, yet another relation of the deceased stepped forward, viz. Dr. H. Lund, and protested against the 'Christian burial' that had been given to his uncle and friend, in spite of the fact that the latter had sundered himself as decisively as possible from the official Church. Lund illustrated his indictments by quotations, partly from Dr. S. Kierkegaard's works, and partly from the New Testament. When the speaker had finished, the Dean said that Lund had no right to speak in the cemetery. The company then dispersed.

From the *Fatherland*, 19 November 1855

3

The Swedish *Evening News* reports Søren Kierkegaard's death as follows: 'By today's Danish post the sad news has come that one

[1] Should be forty-two.

of Denmark's most intelligent and profound thinkers, who is also the greatest religious author in Scandinavia, Dr. Søren Aabye Kierkegaard, has died in Copenhagen at the age of forty-three.[1] His literary work is well known to the educated world in Sweden. We have already given an account of the attack he recently began against official Christianity and its prelatical lords with their coats of arms. The almost incredible activity he has recently displayed has undoubtedly contributed to undermine his already enfeebled health and delicate frame. A few weeks ago news was received that he had been obliged to take to his bed, after a collapse which left a partial paralysis. He passed away quietly in the evening of the 11th.

The passing of such a talented, honest, courageous, and self-sacrificing fighter for truth, will certainly call forth feelings of sorrow in all the three northern kingdoms; though it is possible that some of the prelatical 'witnesses for truth' will take the opportunity to express their satisfaction, and will say that this early interruption of the fight he had begun is to be interpreted as a sign or punishment from heaven.

From the *Fatherland*, 23 November 1855, and also the *Holbæk Avis*, No. 182, 23 November 1855

4

The question of Dr. Søren Kierkegaard's burial occupies many people's minds. We wish to contribute a few words to the question, but we would straightway ask that the burial itself, and the way it was carried out, be kept distinct.

If Dr. Kierkegaard had been taken from the hospital direct to the grave on a weekday, and there had been committed to earth with prayer, that, as it seems to us, would have been right and appropriate. His former devotional writings, the memory of his regular participation for many years in public worship and in Holy Communion, his own preaching of the word from the pulpit, all seem to us to justify such a course; the more so as the outspoken attack of his last years stands in very sharp contrast to these things, and seems to indicate, both in itself, and still more by his death, that he was unbalanced in mind. No human judgement can possibly decide whether or not he was responsible. If therefore the Church, having on the whole taken his very violent attacks calmly while he was alive, should stand up in judgement now that he is dead, and deny him a church burial, then people may very well complain of priestly intolerance.

One can only agree then that the Church's formula should have been used over him as it is over everybody, 'From earth thou hast

[1] Should be forty-two.

come, to earth shalt thou return, from earth thou shalt rise again.' The source of offence lies in the *way* the funeral was arranged. It was conducted from the Cathedral Church of Our Lady, and that on a Sunday. We can readily believe that those in whose hands the final arrangements lay had at first no notion how inappropriate and tactless their action was. But it is very reprehensible that they did not realize it later, since we can state on fully reliable authority that Dean Tryde drew the attention of the clergy concerned[1] very warmly and forcibly to the matter; and this at a stage when arrangements could have been changed. But out of kindly regard for the family's feelings, the Dean would not take the extreme step of prohibiting them the use of the church.

In these circumstances it is doubly hard to understand a most provocative scene by the grave, when a protest was made against the church funeral which had taken place. Many stated that this protest was made, of all people, by a member of the family, the deceased sister's son. We must however refrain from further comment until the matter is better cleared up. But we hope our highly esteemed Cultus Minister will know how to defend the National Church from disturbances in the exercise of its sacred functions: the State ought to be a defence around every religious denomination in the country.

From the *Berling News*, No. 272, dated 21 November 1855

5

It is said that a great many have the intention to leave the Folkekirke[2] in order to form a new religious society in a Kierkegaardian spirit. This is to bear the name 'The Evangelical-Lutheran Church'. Already a prayer-room has been set aside in Broad Street, which will, it is hoped, be consecrated on Sunday. When the time and place are made public, a large crowd will without fail be present—out of curiosity if for nothing else. We will not take upon ourselves here to judge how far such a demonstration against the Folkekirke[2] which certainly rests firm in the constitution—is justified. But we hope there will not be so enormous a breach as there has been, in like circumstances, in two of the world's freest lands—Great Britain and the U.S.A.[3]

From the *Holbæk Avis*[4] No. 181, Wednesday, 21 November 1855

[1] Referring primarily to Kierkegaard's brother Peter, who was in charge of the church service.

[2] Literally 'People's Church'. I leave it untranslated because it sounds odd in English. It is a more homely name for the State Church.

[3] Such a founding of a Kierkegaardian sect was entirely contrary to S.K.'s wishes. Fortunately the attempt failed.

[4] *Avis* means newspaper. Holbæk is a delightful town of (today) 13,000 inhabitants. It is situated on the Holbæk Fjord in the North-west of Sjælland.

6

Last Sunday afternoon at 12.30 p.m. a huge crowd of people streamed out to the Church of Our Lady. Dr. Søren Kierkegaard's coffin stood in the little chapel where formerly Thorvaldsen's[1] coffin had lain.

Death had taken upon itself to force the Church to give an answer, the long awaited answer, to Kierkegaard's attack on the Church. The immediate occasion of this attack was Martensen's misuse of the words 'witness for the truth', in a sermon shortly after Mynster's death. The church was crowded. The coffin was carried (from the mortuary chapel), into the main body of the church, and placed by the steps of the choir. The deceased's brother, Dr. P. C. Kierkegaard, stepped out of the little cortège which with the exception of one person consisted of the deceased's relations. Dr. Kierkegaard gave a short account of the significance his brother had had for his family, whose last representative he (the speaker) there stood. The speaker said he refused to speak specifically to the large concourse which such varied motives had brought to the church. Thereupon he went down to the coffin and in a long prayer asked God's mercy for his brother, and begged forgiveness for his 'perplexed and bewildered soul'.

The coffin was put on the bier, the little cortège rode in carriages, and an innumerable multitude followed on foot; accompanying the coffin of a man whom the nation had long reckoned among its highest people, and above all, as its *own*. The coffin was carried from the hearse by students who had voluntarily offered their services, and it was lowered into the family grave of the Kierkegaards. Dean Tryde, with a discontented air, performed the committal and the earth-casting without a single conciliatory word. When he stepped down from the dais, a young man from the cortège stepped forward to the edge of the grave. Announcing himself as Dr. Lund, Dr. of Medicine, the son of Kierkegaard's sister and a most intimate friend of the deceased, he asked permission to speak a few words. This was given with acclamation. He thereupon reminded the company that Dr. Kierkegaard's articles in the *Fatherland* had had the object of emphasizing the words of the apostle S. John in Revelations, chapter 3, which he then read aloud. 'I know thy works that they are neither cold nor hot. I would thou wert cold or hot. So then because thou art lukewarm and neither cold nor hot, I will spue thee out of my mouth.' The introspective trend of the deceased's teaching (Lund

[1] Bertal Thorvaldsen (1768–1844) was a world-renowned Danish sculptor. The 'chapel' referred to is the mortuary chapel attached to all Danish churches, where the body lies till the day of the funeral.

went on), is in full accord with the Bible. But when, in his paper *The Instant*, Kierkegaard turned against the official Church, he had no less justification and support in Scripture; and he certainly ratified his words by his example. The sharpest complaint he made against the Church is in *The Instant*, No. 2. The official Church (says that article), is making itself ridiculous. The Church does not ask whether a person *is* a Christian, but takes him under its wing *as* a Christian if only he pays the Church for doing so. If a man dies and leaves enough to pay the priest, the clerk and the others, he is buried with the Church's ceremonial, even though, by word and deed, he had repudiated the official Church.[1] What other religious denomination would do such a thing? If a Jew is baptized a Christian, the Jews do not bury him. If a Turk changes his religion, the Mohommedan mullahs do not direct his obsequies. But the official Church does—provided one can pay. In other words, the Church acts for the sake of money. The person buried here (continued Lund) did not leave more than would cover the cost of his burial.[2] Anything else lacking was made up by his family. Although, both by word and deed, he had all his life protested, in a long series of writings, against belonging to the official Church, that Church has taken him and buried him as one of her own—because he could pay. Was the speaker then not right in acclaiming the Church as 'Babylon the great, mother of all harlots and all abominations of the earth?'[3] The speaker therefore protested against this present audacity of the Church in appropriating the deceased, whose life had been a protest against the official Church. The speaker had had no power to stop this offensive ceremony. True he was taking part in it, but only in order to protest against a deed which was against the deceased's wish, and equally against his right.

Dr. Kierkegaard's friend stepped down from the grave amidst silence from the assembled crowd. Then followed a scene, the like of which has not been seen since that passionate cry was heard by Ophelia's grave. Dean Tryde protested against the violation of the Church on its own ground. 'Stop the thief, he is stealing what is holy!' shouted a recalcitrant workman. From many sides people wanted to speak. 'Speak! Speak!' rang through the throng. The police were present in strong representation, and would have forcibly preserved order, but a sensible cry was heard from a sensible person, 'Let us not demean the occasion. Let every honest man now go

[1] This is the gist of what the *Instant*, No. 2 says. The speaker read it out. [Newspaper's note.]
[2] Before his death Dr. Kierkegaard had given away all he possessed to the needy. [Newspaper's note.]
[3] Revelation 17:5.

home.' This turned the scales, and the assembly left the grave quietly and soberly. The whole of this latter incident lasted only a few minutes after Lund's speech was ended.

From the *Holbæk Avis*, No. 182, Friday, 23 November 1855

7

I imagine that only a very small proportion of the readers of this journal have any very wide knowledge of Søren Kierkegaard. He is a man whose name will probably, after his sudden death, come to occupy an important place in the history of the Danish Church. For through the medium of the broadsheets he has lately been publishing, he has unmasked the official Christianity of our times, and shown that it more resembles utter hypocrisy than public worship and veneration of God in spirit and in truth. Naturally this unmasking has struck terror into the hearts of not a few of the Danish clergy. It is therefore a pleasure to me to describe shortly what I know about this—as he seems to me—remarkable man. For it may be of some value for the religious life of our community.

Søren Kierkegaard was a man who lived a retired bachelor life as a theological M.A. He made himself specially famous in his latter days by writing in the *Fatherland* some articles about the meaning of the phrase 'witness for truth'. Even more important were his broadsheets called *The Instant*, wherein he pointed out to all the clergy and also to the public at large, that most of the official Christianity of the present time is so antagonistic to the Christianity of the New Testament, indeed clean contrary to it. It is designed to befool God, who dislikes being regaled with outward ceremonies and forms or official formularies, clichés, and other such pomposities, but absolutely demands of every one who would be a Christian that he deny himself and forsake and renounce the world's false adulations and allurements. Whatever judgement may from different sides be formed about this, it is certain that in his broadsheets *The Instant*, Søren Kierkegaard has shown the public in Denmark that true apostolic Christianity is something quite different from what people are accustomed to learn and hear from many of the clergy. By their state-and-church ordination and the very oath they take, the clergy are committed to much in the State-Church which is clean contrary to the Christianity of the New Testament. Therefore Søren Kierkegaard has taken the opportunity to overturn, I will not say the whole priestly fabric, but certainly the distortions in the State-Church, which, when compared with real, true Christianity, is a mask for vacuity. All this, I imagine, will have the result that a state of affairs so supremely important to our people generally, will not for long bear exposure; but must soon be regulated—and the sooner the better.

In the nature of the case, a person who ventures out so decisively and completely as Søren Kierkegaard did—especially when it concerns a matter that cuts so deeply as religion always does—is not only bound to be exposed to misjudgement and hatred, but also to attempts, by artificial interpretations and representations, to twist and distort the whole literature, so that it all assumes the appearance of being written by a man who is not completely master of his own thoughts and words. So with Søren Kierkegaard! But personalities are often both instruments and media in the service of causes; and we may believe that Søren Kierkegaard was such a personality. Before his death he was destined to help in re-constituting a Church order which today, from the worldly side, is more calculated to provide a thousand good livings than win people to the Christianity of the New Testament.

As usually happens in this world, a man who has performed some great service to mankind seldom becomes really famous and appreciated until after his death. So it will surely be with Søren Kierkegaard. He lived as a man who, to a degree that few attain, was independent of others. He frequently worked quietly and unnoticed in the privacy of his study. But we can see from his writings that he was very religious in his thoughts and ideas; and without doubt he always had a splendid goal before his eyes. Hence, even recently, in his last days, he was destined to win fame by his discussion of a subject which affects the human heart very deeply, namely religion.

We may not share Søren Kierkegaard's views in everything, but it cannot be denied that the above-named broadsheets *The Instant* contain irrefutable truths; and for many centuries there has scarcely been any Dane who dared to tell us such sweeping truths as Søren Kierkegaard has done. This being so, he is almost sure to have stirred up religious feelings in some people, and they will remember him with gratitude. And it may well be that many a person reading the broadsheets has been brought to reflect that official Christianity has perhaps gone astray, and that many a congregation is weighed down by the fact that instead of leading the people into true Christianity, the clergy may be leading them further and further away from it. Let therefore Søren Kierkegaard's words be listened to in our distracted generation, that light may come in the darkness. Well for to us, if we appropriate his words. The fruits will not be lacking.

From the *People's Friend*, No. 7, Friday, 23 November 1855
(*Signed article by the Editor, L. Mortensen*)

8

Dr. Søren Kierkegaard's burial, 18 November 1855.
A Critical Matter For The State Church.

Although this paper does not usually set itself out to deal with Church affairs, it may be assumed that the religious commotion which has been aroused in Denmark through the late Søren Kierkegaard's writings, together with the popular feeling shown at his funeral, a feeling which has been the subject of reflexions in many newspapers, is of a very forceful nature. I have therefore no scruple in presenting the following article, taken from the paper *Letter bearer*. It is so excellently written, compared with what has been said in other papers about the afore-mentioned burial, that it deserves to be more widely known. The article is written by an acquaintance of mine, a layman living in Copenhagen, who was present at the burial. He writes:

'What wonderful times we live in!' So I heard people exclaim when we went home from the cemetery after Søren Kierkegaard's burial. And I think Christians often say the same thing nowadays.

Kierkegaard was a remarkable man. Remarkable too was his burial. We have never known the like in Denmark.

From the paper *Berling News*, No. 272, it seems that our higher clergy have been put in an awkward predicament by Kierkegaard's corpse. They were in two minds whether they ought to give him a worthy Christian and Church burial, or regard him as a heretic (i.e. an apostle of the devil) and refuse it. It seems that Dean Tryde was disposed to refuse burial; anyway the *Berling News* can 'from entirely reliable sources' assure us that the Dean has 'warmly and emphatically' called attention to the 'unsuitability and tactlessness' of burying him on a Sunday, and of having the service in the Cathedral to boot. But 'out of consideration for the family' he would not refuse burial.

So Kierkegaard's coffin stood, decorated with wreaths, in a place of honour on the floor of the Cathedral. His brother, Rector of Pedersborg near Sorø, stood at the entrance to the chancel and spoke over him before the huge congregation of perhaps over five or six thousand people—and many of them could not get in.

The speaker said that he was the only remaining member of the family; that his father in his eighth year, sick and weak, had tended sheep on the Jutland heath; but in his twenty-second year he had become a citizen and hosier[1] in Copenhagen. Søren Kierkegaard had

[1] The term 'hosier' however, came to cover a wide field. The father was in fact a general dealer in a large way.

preserved many of his mother's words in his writings.[1] He had gone far astray in these his latest days, and seemed to want to shake what no power on earth can shake [i.e. the Church]. Unfortunately none of the clergy had had sufficient vigour to take him by the arm for a moment while he was still alive, and there hold him fast so that he could have rested a little. That would have been excellent for him. Not only in Denmark, but in the neighbouring countries too, young folk, middle aged and elderly people—yes and even deluded men—had felt accused and stung, shaken and fearful, by what Søren had written. He wanted the dross removed from the Church. With his lantern he had searched in corners where people would least have expected. Multitudes (said the preacher) were here present in this church, and many more were present in spirit; and amongst these there were many different opinions. Some thought that since a Samson (Søren) had so mightily moved that centuries-old structure, the holy Catholic[2] Church, it must soon fall. But the preacher would remind his audience that God's word and whatsoever is built thereon shall stand, even if heaven and earth shall pass away. He had 'absolutely nothing' to say to the assembly as such. He could not even thank them for coming. The man on the bier, as they knew well, was no friend of crowds and their followers; and he hated all show. So he would pray one prayer, and he invited those who knew how to pray to join with him.

We got the impression—at least I did—that the speaker would have more to say on another occasion; the sort of thing in fact which he did say at a clergy conference in Roskilde, in a paper which he there promised to publish.[3] The fact however that Søren Kierkegaard is now dead will, we hope, contribute towards stirring up and increasing a strong spirit of brotherhood.[4] Above all, may the subsequent words and writings of the deceased's brother not make it too apparent that he is a 'paid servant of the State'. Rather, by God's grace, may there be a cleansing and glorifying such as God's holy and faithful Church here in the North, dearly bought as it is with the blood of Christ, deserves to get through one of her most favoured and gifted believers and servants.

[1] This is a startling statement. If it is true, it means that S.K.'s complete silence about his mother (he makes no mention of her name in his writings) does not imply lack of influence.

[2] The speaker however used the word 'Universal', as the Danes always do, even in the Creed.

[3] Peter made two speeches about Søren at the Roskilde Clergy Convention, viz. 30 Oct. 1849, and 5 July 1855. (See section V below.) Peter expressly says that the latter speech was never published. The former was; so it is the former that is referred to here.

[4] Brotherly affection had been impaired by Peter's speeches at the Roskilde Convention, as will appear in section V below.

At the cemetery—the long road—not very many people were assembled, yet certainly more than at an ordinary funeral. Dean Tryde, Confessiarius, Ridder of Denmark, and Dannebrogsmand (titles and orders which Kierkegaard in his lifetime had so deeply hated and refused), cast the earth upon Søren with the words always used, 'From earth you have come, to earth you shall return; from earth you shall rise again.' He stood for a moment with his hat before his eyes, and then stepped down from the dais by the graveside. A soft, discontented murmur was heard through the company, 'That was bad.' It was as if one heard Wessel's words,[1] 'here rests Peter and nothing more'; only here it was Søren. But the thing was not to end there. Kierkegaard was mightily to revenge himself upon his Philistines at his death.

A young man, sister's son to the deceased, stood forth and asked permission to say a few words. The Dean objected. The people cried audibly, 'Yes let us hear.' Lund[2] [the would-be speaker] therefore spoke his mind. The drift of his speech was that what had been said so far was all beside the point. What Kierkegaard has written stands or falls with him, according as it is right or wrong. His articles in the *Fatherland* were in line with the New Testament. Here he read Revelations 3:14–end, laying special stress on the words 'thou knowest not that thou art wretched and miserable and poor and blind and naked'. He read article 6 from the *Instant*, No. 2. The article is entitled 'We are all Christians.' It shows the State's blunder in wanting to make everybody Christians, even those who are free thinkers and eschew Christianity. Extraordinarily enough, one can be punished by law—for thieving say—and yet remain a Christian, according to the State's idea. Equally when a convicted person dies, if he has enough money to be buried with, then he has to be buried as a Christian. Kierkegaard had declared in his writings that he was not a Christian. (A voice: 'that is a lie'.) He refused to be a Christian of the official sort, where all are Christians. Yet the State Church had done a thing which no other denomination would have done, viz. taken him by force and buried him as a Christian, i.e. as one of its members. But in doing so the Church had profaned its own self and made itself contemptible. For what baptized Jew would at death be buried as a Jew; or what Turk who had gone over to another religion, would at death be buried as a Turk? The State Church was the great whore, with whom all kings and princes of the earth have committed fornication—here he read from

[1] From Wessel's play, *Love without Stockings*.
[2] He was working as a doctor at Frederik's Hospital when S.K. lay there in his last illness. See Section III, nos. 1, 3, 5, 8.

Revelations 18. The speaker himself would follow Kierkegaard's advice. 'Who so does not take part in the official worship of God has certainly one sin the less.' He was only there to protest.

When Lund stepped down, Tryde pointed out emphatically that as a young man he may not know the laws which do not allow an unordained man to make a speech in a cemetery. Lund, however, thought he had the Dean's permission; to which the Dean said No. 'Then I have spoken without permission' replied the other. A young student shouted 'Nobody else is speaking, so let us go home'; and the people obeyed. Yet there was still an outcry from the other side, 'Stop the thief, he is desecrating holy places'; whereupon a violent battle of words took place between individuals, as to which side the guilt lay for 'this scandal'.

Lund has let his speech be published in the *Fatherland*, hoping that other papers would copy it. The *Morning Post* and some other papers have complied; and everyone is justified in asking for it in the paper he reads.

Swedish papers, and also some Danish ones, state that Kierkegaard had inherited from his father about 100,000 Rigsdaler, but had given them away before he died, so that he left next to nothing behind him. Lund also in his speech at the cemetery intimated the same. 'This man,' he said, 'had just enough money to be buried with.' May I therefore ask Lund if this is really so? And if so, why, when he printed his speech, did he omit the words?

The *Letter bearer* has borne faithful witness to this day's remarkable events. I hope therefore that no one will wish ill to that paper or me. The *Letter bearer* could of course have spoken about this affair as our newspapers spoke of the recent festivities on Constitution Day, i.e. so that it was impossible for anybody not present to imagine what took place. But what would that profit the good cause of the Lord? And if there is anybody who does not like this issue, may I console them by saying that in another number they will find something that will be more acceptable.

From the Newspaper *People's Friend*, No. 9, Friday, 7 December 1855

II. PUBLIC AND PRIVATE REACTIONS TO KIERKEGAARD'S ATTACK

1

Letter from Petronella Ross to Professor Sibbern[1]

'. . . . I am reading Mynster's first series of Sermons. But Søren Kierkegaard's devotional and other works are the religious reading I am most fond of; especially now I have got used to him. Strange though he is, the discourses and sermons of others do not easily satisfy me. The man must be a very unusual person. He has certainly made a rod for his own back by that article in the *Fatherland* about Bishop Mynster. Would he were chastised to his profit, as he deserves; but who can bring him back to life again? His wings need clipping a little—nay perhaps a lot—for he gambols quite wantonly up and down in his own philosophical sphere; and as he presses home his logic he is often as unbeautiful as can be. Usually, however, a better spirit permeates his works. I have only read a few—little enough out of the whole mass—but a little of this sort is a lot to me.'

2

Letter from Pastor J. T. Paulli to his friend Brammer, Bishop in Aarhus.[2] 17 February 1855

'We have had a truly dismal time over Søren Kierkegaard's attack on Mynster. It is really *disgraceful* to use Christianity in the way Kierkegaard does, in order to create a disturbance. There is something demoniac in his vanity. Everything he does is deliberately planned. I have noticed for a long time—we used at one time to take walks together—that he regarded himself as the person whose task it was to foster Christianity among us; and I have told him my opinion about the crooked and dangerous element in his literary work. But I never imagined him capable of such conduct as this. Since his last articles were published, I have neither seen nor spoken to him. I long to tell him what I think of him now.'

[1] Undated, but evidently not long after S.K.'s first article in the *Fatherland*. The letter is in the Sibbern archive in Copenhagen University.

[2] Printed in the *Theological Journal* for 1887, p. 486. Paulli was Mynster's son-in-law.

3

Letter from C. J. Brandt[1] *to Peter Kierkegaard, Rector of Sorø*

'. . . . Warlike times these! Has not Dr. Søren Kierkegaard hurled a burning question at the contemporary world? I do not understand him, least of all his own explanation. For when he says that Mynster was a bad fellow, and explains it by saying he was "the cleverest of you all", it would surely be a mistake if Mynster's friends cried their eyes out in sorrow over the injury Kierkegaard has done him. If Dr. Kierkegaard wants, as he does, to waken all the "Christian" contemporary world to life, then I think he has hung his ideal so ridiculously high up under the loft, that one can easily walk under it without having to bend one's neck. That this is so, is I think proved by the fact that—for example here in Copenhagen—people drink a glass and say "devil take me if Søren Kierkegaard isn't right". For it is certainly a mistake on his part if he thinks, as he seems to do, that he has the stream against him. On the contrary, you only meet about one in ten who do not find him right; and that one is either a parson or a female worshipper of the deceased bishop. This result, which is certainly not the one the New Testament would extol, shows there must be something wrong in the reforming attitude he thinks he has to take up.

4

From Fritz Jurgensen's Papers, 3 April 1855[2]

Zahle was here for a few hours today. He has invited me on Thursday to an intellectual 'binge'[3] he is having. There is to be a discussion of Søren Kierkegaard's recent article in the *Fatherland*, in which he literally abuses the priests, calling them shameless scoundrels and Judases. I could not accept the invitation, because Johansen is coming here then. We talked however about this article and Søren Kierkegaard in general.

5

A scurrilous attack in rhyme

A certain theological student named C. H. Thurah published a poem against Kierkegaard in 1855. That same year he sought the permission of the University (Dec. 18, '55) to present a thesis. His petition is singularly bombastic in tone, and fits in with his evident

[1] Brandt, like Peter Kierkegaard, was a Grundtvigian. He succeeded Grundtvig as pastor of the free church at Vartov in 1872; and at the time of writing was head of one of the famous Grundtvigian Folk-High-Schools (see section V, No. 8 below).

[2] A painter and watchmaker (1818–63). Watchmaking was his means of livelihood, but he made his name as an artist.

[3] The Danish word 'Sold' is colloquial. This entry gives a glimpse of the stir and gossip S.K.'s attack on the Church was making.

bombastic urge to defend God, so to say, from Kierkegaard, which he does in a long poem; a poem published, strangely enough, by a respectable firm G. G. Iversen, who also wanted to publish, but never did, Peter Kierkegaard's funeral oration—a very different document, of which more anon. The poem was advertised as ready on 27 September and actually came out on 2 October. (The 8th number of Kierkegaard's pamphlets *The Instant* came out 11 September.) The poem addresses Kierkegaard as a 'bastard child' alluding to the fact that Kierkegaard took up a negative attitude towards marriage in his latest days. It calls him proud and demonic, and alludes to his supposed riches, especially for one who condemns the clergy for taking money; though in fact 'he left nothing but his library' as one of his brothers-in-law puts it, writing to a relation P. W. Lund, on 16 November, five days after Kierkegaard's death.[1] The poem of course speaks of Kierkegaard's attitude to Mynster and to Regine Olsen, and the gossip it all caused; it sarcastically hits at his sense of duty and his conception of himself as a poet. And finally it advises him to go to his father's grave, 'that old whoremonger', and shout 'Here is your bastard child'.

It is all scurrilous enough, and is here mentioned only to show the kind of thing Kierkegaard had to put up with. The last entry Kierkegaard made in his *Papirer* is dated 25 September 1855, before Thurah's poem appeared. But we know that he afterwards possessed Thurah's poem (it is in the catalogue of his books sold by auction after his death), and Boesen, who visited Kierkegaard on his deathbed, writes, 'Oct. 21. Was with him today, only however for a moment, as it was an inconvenient time. He spoke of Thurah and Martensen.'[2] Thurah's book came out on October 2, the day Kierkegaard collapsed in the street and was taken to Frederik's Hospital. Perhaps the book contributed to this collapse. It certainly led some to see Kierkegaard as the martyr-prophet—quite the reverse of what Thurah had intended.

As evidence for this last statement, there appeared an anonymous counterblast to Thurah's effort, entitled *Thurah and Søren Kierkegaard: some remarks by a theological student*. Thurah, says the pamphlet, has brought shame on his own position as a theological student. 'Besides showing a meanness which ought never to characterize such a one, and a coarseness which immediately rouses our indignation, Thurah tries (sic) to be profound and allegorical.' He is inspired by hatred of Kierkegaard, 'the enemy of theologians', and vents his hatred by attacking Kierkegaard's morality.

With surprising haste Thurah replied (in prose) in a little work

[1] See section III, No. 12 below. [2] *E.P.*, IX, p. 597.

dated 6 October. As Thurah's poem had only appeared 2 October, the anonymous counterblast must have appeared between say 2nd and 4th October. Thurah's new effort is entitled *Why just so?* It is a further work of abuse and attack.

6

Such documents are symptomatic of the many reactions to Kierkegaard's attacks. A young ordinand named William Beck tells us that Kierkegaard's strictures almost turned him from ordination. A young man named Niels Ludberg wrote to Peter Kierkegaard, 'Søren Kierkegaard has made many of us young people doubtful; and it seemed to me dangerous to seek ordination without any real urge. I might be tempted, when wanting to marry and become a father, to seek not God's kingdom and his righteousness, but a living.' An article appeared in the *Fatherland* on 20 December 1855 signed . . . r (which is usually taken to be Brøchner) calling upon the clergy to resign their posts as being the only logical thing to do. A certain M.P. named Zahle also urged the same. A clergyman named Bloch said that Kierkegaard had put himself outside the Church and must expect its doors to be closed against him. A Norwegian priest named Lammer in Skien, started a sect of his own and helped Ibsen to fashion his *Brand*, whose principal character, Brand himself, is supposed to be like Kierkegaard, though in fact he is a travesty of him. Naturally the followers of Grundtvig, who stressed the essentiality of the Church, were especially against Kierkegaard. But two persons must be named who were on Kierkegaard's side.

The first was a priest named H. P. Koefod-Hansen. He had written many reviews of Kierkegaard's books, and later directed a fierce attack against Martensen in works entitled *Kierkegaard against Dr. Martensen* (first part finished in October 1855 and published in 1856) and *Søren Kierkegaard against the Establishment* (published in 1857). Towards the end of his life, however, he became a Roman Catholic.

The other was a lifelong friend of Koefod-Hansen named J. N. Lange, also a priest. He tells us (*Letter bearer between Christians*, No. 21, dated 28 October 1857), that when the neo-Hegelian school's attack on Christianity 'fell on his soul like a heavy weight' he had found in Kierkegaard's writings a healing power. In 1849 Lange had been stirred to the depths by reading Kierkegaard's *Sickness unto death*, and that had begun his unswerving attachment to Kierkegaard. Lange declared in a sermon that from then onwards Kierkegaard's thought 'gave his life its characteristic bent'. Like others, however, he was puzzled by Kierkegaard's attack on the Church.

Koefod-Hansen published a volume of Lange's sermons, and in his Preface tells us how 'all of us who had found help and support in Kierkegaard's writings, and thought we had found a sure ground to stand on in the spiritual confusion of our age' were left groping and uncertain again, when Kierkegaard so bitterly attacked the Church. Curiously enough, Hansen and Lange were now included as objects of attack from the very man who had been such a help to them; for both of them were priests. Though unknown to Kierkegaard personally, Lange visited him when the attacks began (i.e. before Kierkegaard went to hospital), in order to try and get to the heart of his meaning. Kierkegaard received him kindly, but would answer his question no further than to say that Lange must try to understand 'by himself' according to his conscience and spiritual power. Nothing more could of course be done after that; yet Lange was one of the few who obtained permission to see Kierkegaard when he lay sick in hospital. A few months later Kofoed-Hansen received some account of what happened by the dying man's bedside. He met Lange in the spring of 1856, and Lange spoke of the deep sympathy he had expressed to Kierkegaard, and said how kindly a pressure of the hand Kierkegaard gave him. A Swedish writer named Rudin tells us that Lange also informed him of a little incident by the bedside. When Lange expressed his thanks to Kierkegaard for the stand he had taken and wished him health and strength again, the sick man had replied that if he wanted to wish anything, he should wish that he might die (Rudin, *S.K.'s person and authorship, 1880*, page 329). What (continues Rudin) made Lange the more upset, was that certain sectarians, who had, for their own reasons, applauded Kierkegaard's attack, tried to get him (Lange) over to their side. Lange was tempted. A private letter written by Lange's son Thor to P. P. Jørgensen (Jørgensen wrote a biography of Kofoed-Hansen; an excellent book), says, 'Kofoed-Hansen disapproved of my father's momentary leanings towards Pastor Grunnet who founded a free Church in Copenhagen. Kofoed-Hansen considered this tantamount to founding a new form of official Christianity.'

But with all his trials, Lange's ardour for Kierkegaard never cooled. He had gathered a band of students around him to study Kierkegaard. One of these, C. F. Leith, who entered the university in 1856 and later became a rural dean, wrote to the above-mentioned P. P. Jørgensen in April 1914 as follows, 'The reason I as a young student joined the circle around Pastor Lange was that even as a schoolboy I had become interested in Kierkegaard, by reading his articles in the *Fatherland*. Lange was, so far as I could gather, the only priest in Copenhagen who clearly and definitely adhered to

Kierkegaard's position. Nobody among the clergy could better interpret Kierkegaard's thoughts than Lange, for all his own life and thought were sustained by Kierkegaard. I felt Lange to be a struggling spirit who passionately wanted one thing only—truth and sincerity towards God. I have not met so downright a religious passion in anyone else. We were four theological students who heard him.' I may add that from the *History of the Danish Clergy, 1884–1911* Vol. II, pp. 253 and 311, it would appear that Pastor Lange was a refuge for other theologians too, during the agitation caused by Kierkegaard's attack on the Church.

Of course all the little journals of Denmark were busy on this Kierkegaard theme—the *Dannevirke*, the *Øresund*, and others. Worthy of mention is the *Letter bearer* which we met above in Section I. The extract there given shows the paper's worth. Its editor, Niels Johansen once tried to call on Kierkegaard during the Attack, but was refused. 'From the time I definitely began my fight with official Christianity,' writes Kierkegaard in his *Papirer* about this time (XI,[3] B, 157), 'my blows have been accompanied by people wanting to see me from all sides. My method is as follows: I do not answer letters. For those who want to talk with me I have one fixed answer, that I cannot discuss things. I use this formula purposely, so as not to offend anyone. That is my eternal desire, especially with the ordinary man. I realize fully that those concerned do not understand me, and so do become offended. That I must put up with; it is not my fault. I cannot and do not need to discuss things with anybody, and if I treat everybody alike that is no offence. . . . When a layman, as for example Niels Johansen, who publishes something he calls *The Letter bearer*, prints a statement that he approached me but was refused, then the clergy probably reckon that that shows me up. When thereupon the same Johansen turns to one of these clerical creatures, who better understand themselves quantatively, he is treated quite differently (and for a different reason perhaps), as one may read in the *Letter bearer*. Hr. Hjorth, editor of the *Evangelical Weekly*, immediately makes him a present of six months' copies of this weekly, and comes into a sentimental agreement with him. Numbers make all the difference.'

III. LETTERS AND DOCUMENTS ABOUT KIERKEGAARD'S LAST ILLNESS AND DEATH

At the time of Søren's last illness, his brother Peter Christian Kierkegaard was Rector of Sorø, forty-seven miles from Copenhagen. This has had the fortunate result for future history, that several letters from relations were written to Peter, and have been preserved. Here are some of them, presented in chronological order. They supplement and intensify what Henriette Lund says, as related above.

1

From Michael Lund, dated 7 October 1855. [Michael and his brother Henrik were both doctors at Frederik's Hospital where Søren lay.]

'Søren's condition is distressing, in all likelihood it is an affectation of the spinal cord, with paralysis of both legs, so that he cannot support himself or keep upright. He lies now in Frederik's Hospital, and all things considered, is content with the treatment and the nursing. Whether his sickness can be cured, it is impossible to decide. One scarcely dare build up great hopes, though we need not give up hope altogether.'

2

From J. C. Lund, father to the above Michael, and Søren's brother-in-law, dated 10 October 1855.

'Your brother is poorly. I doubt very much whether he will get over it, and both Henrik and Michael feel the same; though my nephew Peter[1] has today heard a more favourable opinion.'

3

From the same, dated 16 October 1855.

'I have to report that your brother's condition is very weak. Henrik and Michael, who visit him every day, have given up thinking he can last very long. I myself saw him last Sunday, along with my daughter Sophie, but not since. I was sent away today by the nurse, who said he was very poorly and did not wish to see anybody. So I contented myself with sending in a greeting. But I shall try again

[1] See letters 4 and 6 below.

tomorrow. He is evidently worse than when I last heard from my sons. If you want to see him, then you ought not to delay long.'

Peter responded quickly, visiting Copenhagen on 18 October. He had already, through guests from Copenhagen, learnt of Søren's collapse. He writes in his 1855 diary, '3 October, J. C. Lund and Schou the merchant visited me from Slagelse (after Søren's collapse 26 or perhaps 27–29 September[1]). 18–20 October I was in Copenhagen, after receiving a letter from J. C. Lund. I tried to see him in Frederik's Hospital, but in vain.'[2]

We have already spoken (see Introduction to this Part III), of this sad refusal of Søren to see his brother. We may rightly feel worried about it, but we can take comfort from the following letter, which shows that Søren's feelings were not so personally resentful as may at first sight appear.

4

From H. F. Lund [*Henriette's father, and J. C. Lund's brother, both men having married respective sisters of Søren*]. *Dated 23 October 1855.*

'Dear Peter—I was with Søren this afternoon. I found him in a worse condition than when I last saw him. For his own sake it grieved me greatly that he would not let you go in to see him when you were last here. I told him that my object in visiting him was to beg him to let me send you a brotherly greeting. For I wanted to write to you anyhow. He had not the slightest objection to this, providing it was kept quite distinct from your literary differences. Gladly therefore I send you a friendly and brotherly greeting from him; deeply moved, he took my hand on parting and said, "God be with you." It is my duty to let you know this, and the sooner the better; for I know how upset you were that he could take up the attitude he did. He has I think not many days to live. God give him peace. Thank you for your goodness to Peter.' [H.F.'s youngest son and Henriette's brother. See Letter 6 below, and Introduction to Part II above.]

5

From Carl Lund, dated 24 October 1855. [Carl—see Part II Introduction—was the son of J. C. Lund. He owned an estate or farm in Sjælland.]

'Dear Uncle—As promised, I take up my pen to let you know how I found Uncle Søren. I was with him on Monday afternoon,

[1] This must refer to Søren's first collapse in his rooms, not his final collapse on 2 Oct., in the street.

[2] On this painful refusal, see especially section V, No. 8.

having enquired that morning whether he would receive me. Michael and Henrik had been with him that morning as usual, and he was then very vivacious and cheerful. He sent Michael off with the words "Dismiss! Quick march!" I was therefore quite surprised to find him so crestfallen as he was when I went in to him. He sat in an armchair in a dressing gown, but bowed together, with his head fallen forward, completely unable to help himself. His hands were shaking, and he coughed somewhat. I was with him some time, and he complained of exhaustion and of lack of sleep at night. I remarked that now that the autumn sowing was finished at home, I was able to get away for a bit. He replied that he would soon be leaving here. I understood him fully. He expected to die soon, and he was resigned. He had now become weaker—and yet in a way stronger too. For he perceived that his powers were failing, and that he could not last much longer. I parted with him thinking that his days on earth could not be many. But sick people are apt to be up and down, and so it is with him; for today I found him much better. He was reading the newspaper, and could use his hands better, but his sleeplessness continued, and he suffered with pains in his seat, because of much sitting and lying. But I do not think, from what Henrik says, that there is much hope. His chest is affected, and this in turn affects not only his chest, but also his lungs and back and many other places. So I see nothing left but to hope in the Lord that his last days will be a preparation, by God's grace, for his last journey. Your respectful nephew, Carl.'

6

From Peter Lund,[1] *dated 25 October.*

'Uncle Søren's condition has alas greatly deteriorated, though he is somewhat better again lately. Sometimes he is as vivacious as ever, but his lack of sleep is bound to interrupt this.'

7

From Pastor Gunni Busk, Vicar of Brøndsby Øster, dated 1 November 1855. [We shall meet Pastor Busk again in connexion with the Roskilde Clergy Convention of 5 July 1855, where Peter spoke about his brother. See below, section V, No. 6.]

'I was glad, dear Dr. Kierkegaard, to hear yesterday, when I was in Copenhagen, that you had been to the city; and I imagine you took

[1] Henriette's own brother whom she loved and praises greatly. At this time he was twenty-one years of age and a candidate for the ministry. At thirty he was killed in battle against the Germans (1864) having volunteered as a private. See below, section IV.

the journey to see your brother, who, as far as human eye can see, is sick unto death. May God look upon him in grace, and may He who "suffered for us more than any angel knows", our merciful Lord and Saviour, not let go his soul, but bear it thither where lives the man whom both you brothers have honoured as your godfearing beloved father.

I have—the all-merciful God be praised—a good hope for Søren's soul. And although I doubt not that you also have the same hope, and nourish it by turning to the source from whence all mercy has its origin (even as all fatherhood has its name), yet I cannot help following the promptings of my heart and telling you what so deeply strengthens and uplifts my hope, and fills my soul with cheerfulness, when in quiet prayer I make intercession for your brother, sick unto death, who, like the rest of us, cannot be saved except by God's mercy alone. My hope rests on your brother's words (indicative of his faith): "Pray for me." I got these words yesterday afternoon from Emil Boesen,[1] to whom Søren had uttered them. Coming as they do from a soul so earnest as I take your brother to be (though I have never seen him), and I believe at bottom so sober too, these words are precious to me. Before God's face I have taken them deeply to heart, in order (so far as I can, or rather in so far as God gives me grace), that I may follow their injunction. Søren asked my friend Emil to "pray for him". It may well be that he would deprecate my prayers for him, because he would see in me a servant of the official Christianity, which he hates. But I call the omniscient God to witness that I also hate and abhor it, and according to the best of my knowledge, I fight it.[2] But though your brother may deprecate my prayers, I do nevertheless pray for his soul; even as I desire that others will pray for *my* sins. And I shall do so as long as God hears me and gives me confidence and boldness before his face. . . . So we have hope in God that your sick brother's soul is not letting his Saviour go, nor we ourselves either, nor any soul that says "Pray for me". And, what is fundamental in everything, may He not let *us* go. Nay, thou the Father of our Lord Jesus Christ and of us, thou never takest thy Holy Spirit from us. What then do we lack? God bless you, Yours affectionately, Gunni Busk.'

[1] See section V, no. 7 and section VI, no. 5.
[2] Busk was a Grundtvigian, and Grundtvig had fought, and for a time was ejected from, the official Church.

8

From J. C. Lund, dated 10 November [arranging the funeral before Søren had died]:

'Since it is only too obvious that your brother's condition cannot improve—we cannot hope for it; on the contrary we must rather expect that his powers will not last much longer—I thought you ought not to be left unprepared for the sad tidings which I think cannot be long in coming. This being so, I do not shrink from asking you, for the sake of good order, whether you possess the deed of conveyance for your family grave, or whether you know where the deed is. Henrik and Michael, who have seen Søren daily, find him so much on the decline, that, to judge from his condition the last few days, he cannot last long; for he lays semi-conscious, and today had no interest in anything. I saw him yesterday, and alas I am obliged to confirm the unfavourable opinion of those attending him, about his condition.'

9

From J. H. Paulli, Mynster's son-in-law, to his friend G. P. Brammer. Dated 12 November 1855 [N.B. the day after Søren died. This letter is printed in the *Theological Journal*, 1887].

'He would see nobody, not even his own brother, who has taken this greatly to heart. . . . He must have suffered from a haemorrhage in the brain, be the cause in his writings or be they due to the haemorrhage. On his sick bed he many times expressed satisfaction with what he had done, and he himself fully expected to die.'

10

From Michael Lund, dated 12 November 1855.

'Dear Uncle. What we have long foreseen, and what you have been prepared for by a letter from father sent the day before yesterday, has now happened; and it is my sad duty to inform you that your brother, our good uncle Søren, ended his life peacefully yesterday evening at 9 p.m. His dying may, in a sense, be said to have been protracted, for he lay in a completely unconscious and comatose state for two days, without knowing anyone, and without being able to speak, swallow, and so on. But just because of this unconscious state, his sufferings, I suppose, were not very great; and while his strength was gradually declining, he met the death he so much desired.'

11

From Pastor H. K. Tryde, Rector of Lynge-cum-Broby, south of Sorø. Dated 13 November 1855.

'Dear Dr. Kierkegaard, I heard yesterday in Ringsted, that your brother's long expected death has come. Driving home, I sat and thought how extraordinarily perverse are men's judgements. Your brother is accounted the enemy of the clergy, and today I met many with a certain smug smile, as if the priesthood was now to be left in peace and quiet. And yet all priests who are sufficiently humble must know that they are the better for Søren Kierkegaard's sharp words—better because their eyes are open to the weakness and fragility both in themselves and in their surroundings. By his words, they have been brought to see more clearly than before how they are absolutely nothing in themselves; though at the same time not a single priest worthy of the name has been shaken from his sure confidence in the Church. In this last respect, your brother was no benefactor to any wavering soul who reckoned him as a friend and us as enemies.

Your brother's latest writings gave me many serious hours, for which I thank him in his grave. To one of his writings especially—about empty declamations from the pulpit and all the hollow externality which a priest's constant association with holy things so easily produces—I owe many serious qualms which hit me hard. Had I therefore had to stand by Søren Kierkegaard's grave to speak, I should have said thank you to him, and so possibly would many of the clergy.'

12

H. F. Lund, Henriette's father, writes to his son, Henriette's brother Vilhelm, owner of Annisegaard where Henriette wrote her Recollections. *See Introduction to Part II above. Date 16 November 1855.*

'Dear Vilhelm. I write these lines chiefly to give you and Christiane our latest news about your uncle's death and the decision taken about his burial. You perhaps know already that it was on Sunday evening about 9 p.m. that God called him from this temporal world. In his last days he got some sleep, and the paralysis of his lower half disappeared, but he could not enjoy anything because he could not swallow. He met his last moments in peace and quietness. He was faithful to the Idea to the end, and God took him from a world which was arrayed against him, because he said what he felt to be true. Now he stands before his Judge, and we must all be silent. Already the world is judging him differently from when he lived. People are willing to recognize his outstandingly intellectual gifts, and there is a movement in the city to find out where he is to be buried. Yesterday afternoon your uncle Peter and your cousin Carl came to the city, and we assembled at your uncle Christian's, where we took the decision that the burial should take place from the Church of Our Lady at 12.30 p.m. on Sunday, November 18. I said that you were unable to be present, since the Bedel has to have precise information. Only eight couples can be invited. You know that I had the joy of sending a loving greeting from the deceased to his brother. It was a greeting full of significance at that serious juncture. If anyone mentions the large fortune he left, just let them talk. The truth is that he left nothing except his library, etc. For he disposed of his fortune partly by buying books, partly to keep himself, partly by largess to the needy. It is one sign of God's goodness to him that He spared him from suffering indigence, and from being dependent on the mercy of others.

Ever your sincere father,

H. F. Lund

IV. FROM TROELS-LUND'S MEMOIRS ENTITLED 'ET LIV', pp. 230 ff

(slightly abbreviated and compressed)

Troels-Lund was a half-brother of Henriette, and Søren's half-nephew.

Lund tells us that he was attending confirmation classes in the winter of 1854–5, and was confirmed in April 1855, being then fifteen. It was naturally somewhat disturbing to read in the *Instant*, Søren Kierkegaard's attack on Confirmation as it was normally administered in the Danish Church. Lund's parents were sad about the whole attack on the Church and did all they could to prevent their children being influenced by it. But in vain. 'Father came home every day full of the gossip outside. He spoke guardedly, but naturally our curiosity was aroused. Sometimes the talk burst in on us from outside, as when, during a visit Councillor Svitzer, my eldest brother's father-in-law said, to my great surprise, "Begad! Søren Kierkegaard is about right." And though we did not normally take the *Fatherland*, copies of that paper, containing uncle's articles, did find their way into the house. My brother Peter [see letter from him above, and note there. He was really Troels' *half*-brother] then a third year student, took every copy with Søren's articles in. And when the *Instant* came out, he subscribed to it. Upstairs in his room, where I was a frequent guest, I sometimes had a chance to read these articles. And from conversations with his friends, at which I was sometimes allowed to be present, I got a wholly different impression from that downstairs. There I only heard regret at Søren Kierkegaard's behaviour, sometimes accompanied with heartfelt sympathy for his person from my sister Henriette. Upstairs I heard admiration for the articles and for their author's courage.

'As the summer went on however, this freer view of the affair penetrated below. Not that the viewpoint of the younger folk prevailed, but it was received with friendly toleration by my parents. Much contributed to this. My brother Ferdinand [full brother to Troels, and at this time eighteen years old] entered the University in the summer of 1855, and thereafter, according to our family custom, he was treated as grown-up, and value was attached to his bringing friends into our home. The house therefore took on a youthful colour, for the young were in the majority. I still remember my mother's surprised look when one of Ferdinand's guests, namely his former tutor in Natural History, Hr. Bolling (afterwards a doctor in Ringsted), with the warmth and fervour of youth, praised Søren Kierkegaard's conduct.

'But though our parents did not alter their viewpoint, they did try to understand the young. . . . I was quite often allowed to hear Peter and Henriette talking together. . . . They were sure that though he was against the Church, Søren found strength in doing God's will. But they wondered how it was all going to end. Since the struggle had begun, he had kept more and more aloof from them, so as not to involve them in matters which were beyond them. [See Henriette's *Recollections* above, extract 17 for corroboration of all the points in this context.] He had for example shown concern that my sister should accompany Uncle Christian and his daughter Sophie on a foreign tour. In his old way he had teased them on their departure. But when they came back he had refused to let them visit him all through the rest of the summer. Peter, who saw him one day in the street, thought how ill he looked.

'I was not of course in a position to understand properly the deepest implications of Søren Kierkegaard's action . . . but I thought there must be something in the Church and its teaching which was supercilious, hard, cruel, ungodly; and a lust for power too—all of which things he was opposed to, and pained by. I admired his courage in taking a stand against all this. But I had not got to the root of his objections, as will easily be seen. He fought the Established Church because it gave a tenuous, distorted, and twisted version of Christianity's absolute demands. His charge was—"too little". I had pictured a "too much". Yet I was not wholly wrong, little though I then knew of his writings.

'But he was changed. There was a streak of something new in him. . . . He had always asserted that he was not a Christian, but only a person trying to think honestly. The new factor was that this zeal for honesty was itself a kind of covenant with God. To discharge his part of the covenant was his joy, and an earnest of God's love; and so was more than compensation for all the ill-will his conduct aroused. . . . The Kierkegaard I suddenly saw, seemed to me to lack the two last articles of the Creed [Christ and the Holy Spirit, together with the doctrine of the Catholic Church]. Yet he confidently clung to God's hand in the carrying out of his duty. . . .

'But at home, all the regret and sympathy with Kierkegaard were suddenly given a rude shock by the news that on the 2nd October he had fallen unconscious in the street, and had been taken dying to Frederik's Hospital. Father immediately decided to visit him, and my sister Henriette, who also heard the news and hastened home to communicate it, went with him. Arrived at the Hospital, they were fully convinced of his approaching death. . . . Father was afraid that the sick man might be troubled . . . by the thought of having used up all his means, so that now he was at the mercy of want. He therefore said to him, "Don't worry about money matters. I will see you have all you need. Only rest and let yourself be nursed and get better." The sick man answered, "I have all I want. Everything has worked out excellently. It is like your old kindness and I thank you sincerely."

'My sister dreaded lest she should see traces of his lacerating struggle upon the sick man; or perhaps even of despair because his powers were now failing him. Instead, she met with a happy smile; blessed and care-free as a martyr's when his struggles are ending. Both visitors were struck by the transcendent lustre which streamed from his eyes and his whole being.

'Kierkegaard allowed hardly anybody to visit him except his friend Emil Boesen [see above]. After 20 October Kierkegaard wished these visits to cease. Nevertheless on 25 October Boesen came again, bringing a sermon by Fenger [Chairman of the Roskilde Meeting mentioned above, where Peter spoke against Søren]. The sick man said, "Send it back to him. I don't want it." "But it is only a token of good will. . . ." "Don't let's talk about it anymore. It upsets me terribly." It is easy to understand that this kind of conversation would put the sick man off from seeing even a brother.

'Although visitors were generally turned away, I myself, by wonderful good fortune, visited and spoke with the sick man. My father and Henriette naturally told my uncle Christian of their visit to uncle Søren. Uncle Christian thought he ought to go too; and Søren agreed to receive him—the more so as his son, Dr. Henrik Lund, who was working at the hospital, was untiring in his care for uncle Søren's every need. It was arranged therefore that uncle Christian and his daughter Sophie should go to the hospital one afternoon. . . . Now one of uncle's peculiarities was that he was always thinking about his health. Concern to preserve his health, however, made him a born opponent of everything that could be called sickness. Illness is all due to oneself. . . . His daughter, knowing this attitude of her father, and dreading lest he should talk to his brother-in-law in his usual superior way, brought him to our house in Gammel Torv to ask if anybody would accompany them to the hospital. Nobody volunteered, so at last my cousin, in despair, turned to me and said, "Troels, would you like to come?" I was willing, so off we went.

'I had never been in a hospital before, so I was interested in the place, the hospital dresses, and the fact that the person sought for was not known by name but by room-number. I think this was as depressing to uncle as to me. At length we found the place: pavilion to the left from Bredgade (Broad Street), single room number so and so, passage so and so, first floor. We were announced and bidden to enter. The sick man sat there pale and spare, bowed together in a high armchair. A tired but kindly smile came over his face as he said Good-day to us. When he saw me, I got an extra little greeting from his eyes as make-weight, which I eagerly reciprocated. Uncle Christian began the conversation by asking the patient how he was, and what was really the matter. The sick man replied, "As you see. I do not know any more myself." This aroused uncle Christian to his usual way of thinking and expressing himself. "Now listen Søren," he said. "Your trouble is nothing more than your old ridiculous way of keeping yourself round shouldered. The position you are sitting in is enough to make anybody ill. Straighten your back and get up. Then your illness will be ended, I promise you." The explosion was violent but unpremeditated. Even the speaker felt silent and abashed. My cousin looked down her nose embarrassed. I stole a glance at the sick man, whose eyes were gently avoiding hers, but sought me as the only member of the public present. He answered not a word, but his glance spoke all the more. It radiated through its sadness such a mild forbearance, coupled with a playful, inciting gleam of disarming humour and sense of fun, that it captivated me immediately; and we exchanged glances with a warmth of mutual understanding. And yet there was something in his look which involuntarily kept one at a distance, or rather uplifted and purified. It extended so to say over a whole gamut of nuances, from the sparkling laughter of a mischievous schoolboy to an all-forgiving insight which sees through things and understands. At the same time I realized that things were now changed from what they were. It was as if all the expression had departed from the movements of his emaciated body, even the features of his face, and had gathered with increasing power into his eyes alone. They shone with a soulfulness which made an indelible impression. . . . When I shook hands with him, the others had already turned away towards the door, so that we were so to speak alone. He took my hand in both his —how small they were, thin and transparently white—and merely said, "Thank you for coming to see me Troels. Farewell!" But these ordinary words were accompanied by a look which I have never seen the like of. It streamed forth with an uplifted, glorified, blessed gleam, so that it seemed to me to make the whole room light. Everything was gathered up in the deep light of his eyes: heartfelt love, a blessed released sorrow, penetrating clarity, and a playful smile. To me it was like a revelation from heaven, a streaming forth from soul to soul, a blessing which imparted new courage, power, and responsibility to me. I was silent and reserved when I got outside. I took good care not to disclose what had happened to me. But my thoughts dwelt on it, so that, as with a firm hand, I might correctly grasp and retain it. No one would be able to understand me. A sick man had said ordinary words to me, and looked kindly upon me with a pair of eyes made lustrous through illness. That was all. But for me it was far more. It was a pregnant initiation, a meeting with a glorified spirit ready to depart this life, who straightway became intensely dear to me. It was a short but glorious hour, which in a flash gave me an intuition into what life and blessedness must be like.

'At last, in the evening of 11 November 1855, Søren Kierkegaard fell asleep and found the peace he so earnestly longed for. A practical question which immediately required solving, was what form his funeral should take. He had wanted to be buried in the family plot in the Assistance Cemetery, and had even decided the verse he wanted on the tombstone. But how should the funeral be conducted? Two possibilities were open; either to let the burial take place in complete silence, or—to have a service in the usual manner. The former seemed like dishonouring the dead, as though his life and deeds had better be kept dark. The latter seemed like a farce, which treated God as a fool; for Kierkegaard had labelled the clergy "liars, deceivers, perjurers". Besides, people might say [echoing Kierkegaard's own words], "Not to take part in this, would be to have one sin the less"—Kierkegaard's advice about church attendance in general. The ultimate choice lay with Søren's brother Peter. He chose to let the funeral go forward in the Church of Our Lady on a Sunday, and he himself would speak. As might be expected, the church was filled to capacity, with a very mixed throng. The first two pews were reserved for the family, who came in very good time and took their places. Father and Uncle Christian, together with the eldest male cousins and brothers, sat in the first pew. By pure chance, I sat alone in the next. A man whom I afterwards came to know as Professor Rasmus Nielsen[1] came and sat beside me, and shut the door so firmly that it locked itself. So we sat sheltered, while the mass surged, pressed, and elbowed together in the middle

[1] A man who associated himself with Kierkegaard's views, but whom Kierkegaard did not wholly trust. See my translation of Hohlenberg's *Søren Kierkegaard*, chapter XI.

aisle. Things were not, as it seemed to me, altogether tranquil, and from time to time I secretly exchanged a glance with my sister Henriette, whom I discovered up in the gallery [see Henriette's *Recollections* above, paragraph 17]. All at once there arose a still stronger movement, with more pressure than hitherto. I feared it was some of the excited-looking people present surging forward to remove the coffin. But I read in my sister's look—and she could see all over the church—that something good was happening. It was a procession of students making their way forward to form a cordon round the coffin.

'Uncle Peter's speech was forceful, and he was not interrupted by any brawling or interference. I heard afterwards that my sister thought it good. I myself understood little of it and remembered nothing. From the church we drove to the cemetery at walking pace, following the hearse. When we alighted, the place was thick with people, and I saw the coffin borne forward with difficulty along the path up to the grave, straight and broad though the path was. All around, the dense multitude, spilling over railings and graves, were thronging to the common rendezvous. I was separated from my relations, made my way alone to the grave, where the excavated soil formed a yellowish grey mound to the left of the removed railings. Here there was less of a crush than I should have expected; I, however, stood in a spot so concealed, that I could see nothing of what went forward, and I was anxious as to how all this discomfort was going to end. It seemed endless. They pushed and thrust against the yellow-grey mound. Then suddenly someone from among them broke loose, pushed forward and stood to the fore. He was a tall young man in black. He took off his hat, looked around with an exceedingly ardent and fervent glance, and shouted over the heads of the throng, "May I ask permission to speak?" Then I recognized him. It was my beloved big cousin Dr. Henrik Lund; he who had always been so jolly, and so good natured and understanding towards us younger folk. He had not long before written to me from Paris, enclosing a sketch of one of my tin soldiers that I had once loved so much. Lately he had been tending and nursing Søren Kierkegaard in hospital, where he was working. I shuddered to see him get up to speak in circumstances such as these. The multitude at once became quieter. "Who is this?" they asked around. "I am Henrik Lund, the Doctor," he answered. "Hear him," came a cry from one quarter, "he is a good man. I have been under him in hospital. Let him speak."

'So he began something like this: "The man who is buried today with full ceremonial, as though he belonged to the Church, was in life the Church's most eager opponent. Only by a trick has the Church appropriated him, and tried to thieve him after his death. But witness shall be borne here by his grave . . . etc., etc." In Kierkegaardian phrases he then pointed out the opposition between the deceased and the Church, and ended by lodging an objection to what had happened there that day. When the speech was over, there was some sporadic and weak applause. The majority however, stood in tense silence, wondering what would happen next—riot, uproar, something extraordinary? But nothing happened.

'The speaker was gone. The big man from the church pew, Rasmus Nielsen, whom I had re-discovered near the grave, and who I think would have liked to speak now, went off, I saw, with an air of vexation. People were beginning to tire of waiting. A few grave-diggers appeared. A laugh was raised when some half-tipsy fellow shouted to a comrade, "Let's go home, Georgie!" I slipped away through the crowd, past the trodden graves to the waiting carriage. I became aware now that it was cold, and I was frozen. I managed to find the carriage. Father and uncle Christian were sitting in it, and I slipped in with them. They were silent and out of spirits. At home, mother had done her best for us. I still remember how the hot soup revived us. Nevertheless the mood continued to be somewhat depressed. All were upset at cousin Henrik, who had been rather emotionally influenced by Søren Kierkegaard's thoughts, and had gone further out than he could steer. I heard to my surprise that his conduct was punishable as disturbing lawful order and the quiet of the cemetery. Moreover all were very sorry for uncle Christian, Henrik's father, for he was very upset at what had happened that day. And it must have been awkward for Peter Kierkegaard too, for he was staying with uncle Christian during his visit, and would meet his nephew Henrik there.

'The ensuing days, far from quenching and softening this depressing mood, rather increased it. Henrik Lund felt himself the inheritor of Søren Kierkegaard's thought, and in duty bound to propagate it further. Some days after the funeral he published a little broadsheet in the style of the *Instant*. It was entitled *The next Instant; what now?* It was, I need hardly say, only a weak echo of Søren Kierkegaard. He soon realized that he was not equal to the task. Excited and overdriven as he was, he decided to follow his Master into death. When his father unexpectedly called on him one morning in his flat, he found him almost unconscious with severed veins. Quickly he called in the doctor and took the poor man to his paternal home. With tender nursing he gradually came to himself, weak though he was, yet relieved by the loss of blood. His father, with loving solicitation, was at pains to find him a house in the country, at Søllerød,[1] where he later—after a brief visit to the West Indies[2]—built up a considerable practice as a skilful and respected physician.

[1] A village some twenty-one miles north of Copenhagen.

[2] Regine Schlegel, *neé* Olsen, Kierkegaard's former fiancée, lived in the Danish West Indies, where her husband was Governor. We are not told which islands Henrik visited, but it appears from what Regine tells us that he did not visit St. Jean, where she then was. See below, section VI, No. 5.

V. PETER AND SØREN

1

From Peter's Journals

(a) *June 1855.* Søren's *This has to be said* and Nos. 1 and 2 of *The Instant* belong to the past months and have been occupying me—but N.B. only in my thoughts—and after a fleeting glance at them and at many (but not all), of the articles in the *Fatherland.*[1]

(b) *June 1855.* Was in Gentofte on 7 June, and at 4 p.m. was present at the wedding of Vilhelm Lund (Peter's nephew) and Camilla Schwitzer.

(c) *July–August 1855.* Spoke against Søren's pseudonymous literature and its theories, at Roskilde Clergy Convention on 5 July.

(d) *In August 1855* we gather that Peter was for ten days at Annisegaard and at Copenhagen.

(e) *October 1855.* Entry already quoted, section III, No. 3, p. 101.

2

From Peter's Collected writings, *Vol. IV, p. 123*[2]

A suggestion I put to Søren in the summer of 1855 [it would seem likely that this was on one of the occasions (b) or (d) mentioned above, i.e. in June at the Gentofte wedding, or in August when visiting Annisegaard and Copenhagen], that he should go away for a time, he evaded shortly and brusquely with the words, 'Is this a time to go away?'—if I remember rightly. And to a large extent this was justified, because there were some things it had long been our custom not to discuss, and this certainly made me refrain from telling him quite freely and fully why I gave him this advice. I can quite see that without such an explanation I might well seem to be advising him to run away from the fight.

A second suggestion I made to him later was also refused, and it occurred to me *later*, though I did not notice it straight away at the time, that for so trenchant a dialectician as he usually was, he seemed then very languid. This suggestion was that we should discuss together some of the main points wherein his efforts seemed to

[1] See Introduction to Part III supra.
[2] Written in 1881, twenty-six years after the events they describe.

me to be misdirected. We were both aware, I said, how far I was from agreeing with much of his viewpoint and utterances, and we had long been silent about this, without any insincerity. Now, however, I was willing to talk with him.

3

From the same, p. 120

Introductory note by Peter. The following communication was written 14–16 March 1881, when there came a representation to me which led me to suppose that something of this sort would be included at the end of the last volume of Søren Kierkegaard's *Posthumous Papers.* The first edition of these, by Pastor Barfod, came out in 1869–1881—but the publisher decided against including it.

I have often been asked since the death of my famous brother Søren, whether I could not bring myself to relate at least the straightforward outer facts concerning the three occasions when, partly during his working period and partly immediately afterwards, I spoke about him in public. It was thought that I was in some measure called to, nay almost bound to, let a definite message concerning these occasions be published, so that the many loose and confused declarations about those ocasions (for example those accounts which, especially in the period immediately after his death, were disseminated through the newspapers), might not be transmitted to posterity uncorrected and unopposed, there to be retained as a true account of this side of the affair. In the confused period shortly after his death, I admit I sometimes felt myself prompted to attempt to make a statement. But I soon learnt that I must give up the idea, and align myself to the words of the Psalmist, 'I was like a deaf man and heard not; and as one that is dumb, who doth not open his mouth.' For I felt more and more strongly, with every attempt I made, that I could not, shortly, concisely, and quite objectively, give the necessary clarification, in face of the reports and judgements which came out in the *Instant*-literature. For only partially and under constraint, did I wish to acquaint myself with it all. It would have been more than I could endure, to get involved in disputes as to its rightness. Later there were many other hindrances which I need not touch upon here. But now, when Søren has been dead a full twenty-five years, I have been asked again, and this time it is almost like a demand. Since his literary remains are to be published in the complete form in which they will be delivered to posterity, and the edition is almost completed, I must no longer refuse, or evade agreement. Let then the attempt be made, under the strict condition that what is here given be regarded as a straightforward, objective account.

4

From the same, p. 121.

Peter's first speech at the Roskilde Convention, 30 October 1849

It was then first at the Roskilde Clergy Convention held in Ringsted 30 October 1849 that I came to speak publicly about the rich literature which Søren has given to the reading public of Denmark. And this happened—as may be seen from the report in the Danish *Church Times* for 1850, p. 171–193[1]—in an all-but extemporary speech, in which I used the text II Corinthians 5:13, 'Whether we are beside ourselves (literally "ecstatic" ἐξέστημεν[2]): it is unto God; whether we are of sober mind (σωφροσυνοῦμεν) it is unto you.' I tried first to interpret the words in their context, and then to use them so as to show the difference between Søren's position and that of Martensen's *Dogmatic*. I said that ecstasy was by and large the characteristic of Søren, calm of Martensen. But I dealt chiefly with Søren, and only used Martensen to offset what I said; as any reader of my speech may see. Nevertheless, when the article was printed, and so I suppose came to Søren's knowledge, he was displeased. I know this from his own mouth, and I understand it much more fully now, seeing it in conjunction with his whole position and polemic. There was never any real discussion about these things so far as I remember; indeed it had been our custom for many years not to discuss his writings when we visited each other, or how far I agreed with him or not—though *he* would often speak forcibly and vividly about his plans, intentions, and personal status etc., all in spite of my silence. There was once a time when we *had* discussed our differences; but ever since then we had both recognized that my silent listening meant neither approval nor agreement. He entrusted himself to me as to a confidant, though I lacked one of the two conditions for being that (namely agreement) and only possessed the other (namely silence). Whether after his displeasure at my Convention speech aforementioned, he gave up the kind of confidences I have spoken of, I do not now remember, for I confess I am not a sharp observer. When however I think back to the years immediately

[1] This report is now printed in full in Peter's *Collected Works*, IV, p. 99 ff.

[2] The words τοῦ φρονεῖν or τῶν φρενῶν, or some such words virtually meaning 'the mind' are usually added by Greek writers. The Danish Bible of 1931 renders it 'were outside ourselves' (var ude af os selv). The Danish Bible I think Peter would normally use says 'did not keep calm' (ikke hole Maade) and this is about what Peter means, though he transliterates and uses the word Ekstasen. We can the more understand Søren's indignation I think, if we remember all this Greek background. The word 'beside oneself' or ecstatic, is used of Jesus by his friends (Mark 2:21) and of St. Paul by Festus 'Paul thou art mad' (Acts 26:24).

following the speech, I seem to remember that there were still more of these outspoken and so to say soliloquy-like conversations with me about his intentions, about secret opposition to his struggles and so on, than in former years.

5

Søren's reaction to the above speech

There are five illuminating references to Peter in Søren's Papers for 1849. The first and last are already translated in Dru's *Journals*, but I have re-translated them, and also added the other three. The first is of a general nature. The others all refer to the speech itself.

(a). *Entry I is from Papirer*, X^2, *A*, *134* (*Dru No. 987*).

There is some truth in a remark Peter once made, that the difference between him and me with regard to religion is that he stresses God's love to man, and I man's love to God. The distinction was not wholly new to me. I had often pondered whether God is not too infinitely high for man to dare to love him. Yet it is written, 'Thou shalt love the Lord thy God.' Moreover I have always asserted that it is God who does everything for me.

But the difference between us two is not badly described in this way. The fact is that Peter has never been young in a spiritual sense. His view of religion is unhealthy. He is so anxious and afraid before God, that he remains in a perpetually pusillanimous state. Heaven knows whether he ever gets sufficiently fired to believe boldly that he really *is* loved by God. I, on the other hand, have never been young in a physical sense, but spiritually I *have* been youthful, in a good sense. Overwhelmed by God, and reduced to being less than a sparrow before him, I have nevertheless been given a certain youthful courage which dares to approach Him quite unrestrainedly. Child-like I have been able to perceive that God's very infinity meant that he could be concerned with the very smallest things. Child-like I could enter with devotion into the idea that he would not take it ungraciously if I said, with regard to any honest endeavour, 'Please, please do not slight me O thou infinite one, although in another sense I am, for all time, less than nothing before thee.'

This is youthfulness. It is child-like. But truly it is part of my very being. It has been a blessedness to me that I could so naturally and earnestly and completely understand that—shall I say that the more infinite a being is, the less he can concern himself with small matters? No; I have never been so 'understanding' as that. The more infinite a being is, the more he can and will concern himself about small matters. I have taken it to be literal truth that he concerns himself about every sparrow. . . . There is no small difference between being a child or youth [like me], and having begun straight off with the attitude of old age [like Peter].

(b). *Entry II: Papirer, X², A, 256.*

About Peter

So Peter must needs hold forth about my authorship. What is my reaction? I know for sure that he has only read some of my books *passim*. That, look you, is enough for him. (N.B. He told me this himself.) He had already undertaken to give a lecture at the Convention. But what happens? The lecture he had prepared was not used—for it occurred to him the evening before, 'You could say something about Martensen and Søren and Rasmus Nielsen.'[1] So this speech was given and thereafter printed.[2] If you were to point out to him that it was given without any real knowledge of my work, the answer would be 'Yes, but bless us, this was only for an address to the Convention.' Then why should it be printed? And not only so, but just because the speech was delivered and then printed, it acquires a greater kind of significance than it really has.

How sad! In so small a country as Denmark, where I am not so much as reviewed, everyone uses my writings as an opportunity to say something. My cause retreats rather than advances. There is of course 'not time or place' to embark on all my subtle concretions of the problem in hand. So I am reduced to a gibbering platitude-monger, which means I almost might as well not have written.

And then the distressing fallacy that he is my brother 'who must therefore have the best knowledge!'

(c). *Entry III: Papirer, X², A, 263.*

What would Luther say I wonder about the theory that Peter has advanced to adorn his bleating, 'One should witness for the truth but not against the evil.' By this theory I am to be condemned. No matter if the evil is so shrewd as to ignore our knowledge of the good, perhaps even so audacious as to make capital by saying approvingly, 'You must not dare to witness against the evil lest you tempt God.' In that case, nearly every one of the Church's martyrs is to be judged guilty of having tempted God.

Rather, one tempts God by making such theories; for they con-

[1] Peter expressly told the Convention that he had prepared one speech (of which he gave his audience a resumé), but used another. 'I ask pardon,' he says, 'for offering you something I only thought of yesterday evening. It is but little and hastily prepared.' *Collected Works* IV, p. 101.

[2] The speech was first published in the *Danish Church Times* of 16 Dec. 1849 (No. 219).

For Rasmus Nielsen, see Troels Lund's Recollections above, and also Hohlenberg's *Kierkegaard*, chapter XI.

ceal our lack of courage, faith, and confidence. Surely if by rushing rashly forward we tempt God, we equally do so by shrinking away and staying at home when God expects us to be out in the fray. Is not this to tempt God's patience? Take a picture. Would Napoleon be more angry if a general ventured out on his own, than if he prudently refrained—aye or *im*prudently or irresponsibly for that matter. The greatest merit pusillanimity can attain, is in the last resort, to sleep—so as not to sin or tempt God.

(d). *Entry IV: Papirer X*^{2}*, A, 273.*

Peter's speech at the Convention

It is surely something like confusion-mongering to take that text of St. Paul and point to Martensen and me as representing respectively the two types of life spoken of in the text. For if you compare Martensen with Paul, then Paul is entirely (even his *σωφρόσυνη*) ecstasy. Martensen's and Peter's conception of soberness is a, to some extent, irreligious conception. It represents what is commonplace and easy-going. It should have been pointed out by Peter that in our days it is very difficult to set forth what ecstasy is. For mediocrity, worldly prudence, or whatever you like to call it—this is what counts nowadays. Futhermore, Peter might have pointed out that what characterizes my ecstasy is that it carries just as much soberness in it as ecstacy. Compare how I use pseudonyms, fanciful people (and it is therefore not I that is speaking) to represent ecstasy; while in my devotional discourses I myself speak, quietly and gently. Peter could have pointed to the category The Individual as used by the pseudonyms, and as used by me. And so on.

Yet what does Peter care about all this? With self-satisfaction and of course with the acclamation of the country parsons, he proclaims this commonplace: 'There are two propensities (that is that achieve something), but each is one-sided. But we, we who achieve nothing, we are of the truth. And we are the majority. Believe me, I know we are. Should I not know it? I am eight years older than my brother'.

(e). *Entry V: Papirer X*^{2}*, A, 275 (Dru No. 1013).*

About Peter

I have existed quâ author all this time, and Peter has found no occasion to speak. But scarcely does it seem as if people want to point to me on a bigger scale, than he gets busy to unburden his mind—probably on behalf of the Grundtvigian party [to which he belongs] but also to make a bid for me. His eagerness is also increased I imagine, by having this long-wished-for opportunity to attack Rasmus Nielsen (a very profitable task at the moment) and to hold him up as an example of discipleship—he (Peter) who has been a disciple and copyist of Grundtvig to the extent of ridiculous affectation!

The whole thing has upset me terribly. And Peter has been completely without sympathy during all the time I have suffered the persecution of the mob. I have literally never heard a word from him by mouth or pen concerning this. We have never been very close to each other; but from that time onwards he had held himself entirely aloof. He knows also that I am worried about my finances —but never a word about it.

At last he sees his opportunity. He takes a 'higher position' than the two types—Martensen and S.K. For admittedly he protests that he is not 'mediating', yet in fact it is essential to his thesis. He only uses these two types; therefore he is of course a higher type. (Yet note this 'higher type's' curious words. He says he will not mediate between two sinful persons, which means in ordinary parlance 'I, a sinful person, will not undertake to mediate between two other sinful persons'.) In a popular manner he hits out with all the careless jargon of the day, which is of course capable of dismissing in half an hour the work of seven years. Vigorously he proclaims the supremacy of the country parson and the sovereignty of mediocrity; shielding himself carefully behind the excuse that his speech was a hurried piece of work. He takes the opportunity to use this deception:—'I as the author's elder brother ought to know'—which is the most frightful untruth; untrue to such an extent that he certainly ought to underline it! He ties my hands for I cannot move to reply without the world shouting 'Scandal'. Yet no doubt he thinks he is not being unfriendly, for this is quite a favourable speech he is making about me—which again I have to suffer for in a way, else people will say I am prejudiced. He puts me in difficulties with Rasmus Nielsen too, for Nielsen may think I am behind Peter's attack on him. Conversely, when Nielsen attacks Peter, then I suppose Peter will think I am behind Nielsen. I do not mean that Peter had thought all this out clearly. But to some extent it ought to have been obvious to him, and indeed would have been obvious, if he were not so wont to be very pleased with himself among these country parsons and conventions; so wont that he may even perhaps have thought, in a stupid kind of good-natured way, that he was impartial enough to compliment me. Yet he does not understand that in order to do *that*, he should set a standard and really elucidate my work, and not be hoodwinked by the numerical assessments of men, and his deceits.

6

Peter's second speech to the Roskilde Convention, 5 July 1855

From Peter's Collected Works, *IV, p. 124*

During the Roskilde Convention's summer meeting, 5 July 1855, the Chairman, Ferdinand Fenger, spoke of Søren's recent activities, [Søren's attack on the Church then in full swing.] The Convention, after a short speech by the present Rural Dean of Ringsted, Dr. Andersen, did not seem particularly anxious to deal with this topic, However, at the request of Gunni Buck [see section III letter 7 above], to which the company agreed, I found myself giving a talk on what I felt to be the chief characteristics permeating Søren's writings; which writings were then as good as completed. This second lecture (of which an account is promised in the *Danish Church Times* for 1855, p. 592), was never written down by me; and, so far as I know, none of my hearers have anywhere given any epitome of it. The contents of this speech (for I only *began* the attempt to write it down) I cannot reproduce. My notes were interrupted by a protracted illness, during which I learned that Søren was attacked by his last illness. Nor can I reproduce the speech from memory, as I have often been able to do with other speeches, even some time after their delivery. Two things, however, I feel sure I can mention correctly. *First* I am certain that just as I began my Roskilde speech by unfolding a passage from II Corinthians, so this time I began with a text from I Corinthians 1:22–24, about the Jews asking a sign and the Greeks seeking wisdom, while the Apostle preaches Christ crucified as the power of God and the wisdom of God. Unfolding my theme, I tried to show what had long seemed to me to be rather incorrect and misleading in the way Søren conceived and used his two main theses—one about the Paradox of Faith, and the other asserting that suffering is the Christian's lot. I was obliged to think the latter was more evident in his later works.[1] *Next*, I recall that I ended my address by saying that Søren

[1] Everyone will understand that I am obliged to refrain from attempting even a very short account of what I actually said in detail. This is not only because of the time of suffering and strain, both bodily and mental, that, as I noted above, came upon me before I could get what I said written down, but for another reason also. The passage I Corinthians 1:22–25, I had last used in 1842 (Nov. 11) when I was ordained priest by Mynster. I used it as the text of my ordination address; which address was not without reference to the prevailing Hegelianism. Both between then and 1855, and more especially between 1855 and now, the text has been so often in my thoughts and utterances that it would be altogether impossible for me to say how I treated it in that Roskilde speech. I should almost certainly mix with it something—possibly much—which was not there on that occasion; indeed which I perhaps had not even thought of then. It seems remarkable that I should find myself using this text from my ordination sermon in a public speech during that stormy time after Mynster's death; which death as it were rang in the storm. Mynster had felt obliged to tell me that my delivery of the ordination speech was so hurried that he had taken in none of it! [Peter's note.]

had given us the themes he so forcibly developed in his writings, largely through the pseudonymous mouths of various well-defined and characterized persons or points of view. One might almost be tempted to think that even what was signed 'S.K.' might not for certain be his final words, but only a point of view.

7

Søren's reactions to this second speech of Peter.

To get Søren's reactions we must first turn to his death-bed, where he was visited by a certain Pastor Boesen,[1] priest at Horsens in Jutland. The two had been intimate friends from boyhood, when their repective parents took their families to worship with the Moravian Brethren. Boesen came all the way from Horsens to Copenhagen to act as pastor to the sick man. At the request of Herr Gottsched (collaborator with, and at his death successor to, Pastor Barfod, who produced the first edition of Kierkegaard's *Papers*), Boesen has left an account of his visits.[2] Among other things, Boesen asked the sick man, 'Have you not been angry and bitter?' 'No,' replied Kierkegaard, 'but worried and saddened and made indignant to a high degree—for example by my brother Peter. I did not receive him when he last called on me after his speech at Roskilde. He thinks he is the elder and therefore takes precedence. . . . I have written a piece about him, very sharp. It lies at home in my desk.'

This is probably the 'piece' printed in the *Papirer*, XI³, B, 155. It is too long to quote in full, nor is it necessary. It begins bitterly, 'So then it is from the clergy convention that a deadly blow must needs come. First Bishop Martensen, then Paludan-Müller, then Victor Blok, then Dr. Zeuthen.[3] Now it is from the Convention, especially from the Grundtvigians, and especially from my brother.' Mynster, Søren recalls, was at least one with him in not thinking much of the achievements of the Roskilde Convention! Søren repeats that Peter, though his brother, 'only knows what everybody else may know from my writings, about my inner life.' He again upbraids Peter for characterizing him as 'ecstasy', 'almost joining the crowd in dubbing me "mad"—though he does not say so outright. His considerateness, however, was of a curious kind (not that I mind in the least, for I am completely satisfied that I am meant to be sacrificed), so that even the Grundtvigians' own Journal does not agree with Peter; which is saying a lot for Grundtvigians.' Søren

[1] See pp. 50, 97, 104, 133.

[2] *E.P.*, IX, p. 593 ff.

[3] All these, except Blok, are mentioned in Lowrie's translation of the *Attack on Christendom.*

again complains of Peter's silence during his (Søren's) sufferings—this time his latest sufferings. 'Peter's "considerateness" did not lead him to say a word on my behalf when I suffered through attacking Martensen. . . . He does not meet me man to man, but under cover of a company of people in a Convention. Perhaps my opponents may think a speech like Peter's may make me relent. But the cause I have the honour to serve is the greatest Denmark has ever had. It is nothing less than the future of Christianity, and it must begin here.' Perhaps Peter is brought in, in order to whittle down the whole thing to a quarrel between two brothers. 'We shall see how that works!' adds Søren bitterly. 'But I tell him short and straight that he has acquired an importance he does not really possess, through the aid of these little speeches and party meetings. "Scandal, Scandal", his friends will cry. But I am not afraid of scandal. The New Testament constantly uses this word in respect of Christianity (σκάνδαλον).'

8

What are we to think?

That there is much bitterness in Søren's heart, as revealed in the above, is clear. And it is hard sometimes to excuse it. But let us remember that he is 'expectorating' (to use his own word) or 'getting things off his chest' in private, very largely. What he writes in his *Papirer* does not necessarily represent what he would say in public. Forthright emptying of our thoughts in secret may be good for us. But we need not take all that is said at face value. Even the painful refusal of Søren to see his brother (especially on his death-bed) must be offset by what H. F. Lund tells us (see section III letter 4 above), about the brotherly greeting the sick man sent.

The mitigating facts are I think these:—

(I). Older children do sometimes impose on the younger; or anyway the younger think they do. Søren's study of German romantic literature seemed to Peter, and to his father also, misguided. And certainly this study largely coincided with what are sometimes called Søren's 'wild oats periods', though it is not proved that the sowing was very bad. Peter evidently tried to bring Søren to order, but without effect. Søren criticizes hum-drum people like Peter 'Their standard of morality is like a short epitome of police notices. The most important thing for them is to be useful members of the state, or to hold forth at the club in the evening. . . . These respectable people's love for God appears when their vegetable life is most active, when their hands are folded comfortably on their stomachs, and from their heads, reclining in soft armchairs, with drowsy glances are lifted toward the ceiling, toward higher things. When they speak of bringing up children they mean by well-brought up children, trained monkeys' (*Papirer*, II, A, 127, 128).

For many a year afterwards Søren lets his pseudonyms pour scorn on 'respectable humdrum citizens, who regard it as life's serious business to become something—a right reverend, a father, a "bird king",[1] to be married, have children, have the gout, be an examiner in theology, member of parliament, or even a public executioner.' (*Postscript*, p. 489 = *Værker*, VII, p. 541.)

No doubt this is all self defence, but it does show that Søren believed himself to have a deeper sense of values than these people. And this he had acquired to some extent by the very studies they would condemn.

(II). Both Peter and Søren speak of the reserve between them. This would be particularly exasperating to an open nature like Søren; and any open nature would endorse this. To have a brother who never said a word in all the sufferings he went through, and who would not even discuss his writings, was indeed hard for Søren; especially in view of Peter's superior moral attitude. But Peter was a good man and held important positions. He was at one time Cultus Minister in the Govenment and he became a Bishop. But he was very full of religious scruples all his life, as Søren says. The latter part of his sad and heavy life specially shows this. He never seems to have had Søren's gaiety.

(III). Peter became a confirmed Grundtvigian, and Søren severely criticizes Grundtvig. (See e.g. *Postscript*, Chapter I; though elsewhere this criticism crops up constantly.) Grundtvig was a great patriot, and his presentation of Christianity very 'mixed'. His teaching laid much stress on Nordic mythology (which he made a special study of), in order to show what excellent stock the Danes came from, and so encourage their national spirit when they were likely to be cowed by the Germans. He founded too the famous People's High Schools for adult education, which still flourish and are the admiration of all educationalists.

Grundtvig is now acclaimed by the Danes as one of their greatest men. He made what he called a 'matchless discovery', viz. that the Bible alone will not suffice as the criterion of Christian truth. What is needed is the 'living word' of the Church down the ages, and Church teaching is summed up in the Creeds. Grundtvig even went so far as to declare the Creeds to be in effect the very words of Christ himself. This emphasis on the Church sounds very catholic, but in

[1] The name given to a member of a shooting club who hits the popinjay.

fact it is not so. Grundtvig wanted the Church to include everybody, and to represent the nation on its religious side. To keep a place for everybody in the Church, Grundtvig was prepared to 'accommodate' its demands; and that for patriotic as much as Christian reasons.

All this is of course precisely what Kierkegaard was opposed to. His whole attack on 'Christendom', that is the idea that 'we are all Christians' just because living in a particular geographical area, is completely alien to his thoughts. 'Be ye perfect' is the demand of Christ, and this Søren would hold out for. He wanted Christianity 'neat'.

It is an age-old dilemma. Peter tells us (see below at the end of this section), that one should not lay the strict demands of maturity upon everyone, for fear of alienating people from Christianity; and that, by and large, is the attitude of the Roman Church. Peter would moderate, Søren would confront. And that is at the heart of their difference.

9

Peter's third speech: the funeral oration at Søren's burial, delivered in the Church of Our Lady, Copenhagen, on Sunday 18 November 1855.

From Peter's Collected Works, *IV, p. 125.*

Of the third speech, given before Søren's coffin in Our Lady's Church, I must mention that I have no notes, apart from the visiting card on which, according to my custom, I had previously indicated for myself some of the topics to be touched upon.[1] With the help of these notes, and also of a somewhat unfriendly and clumsy epitome which appeared in one of the contemporary newspapers, [see e.g. section I above, Nos. 6 and 8] and relying too on my own memory, I think I can roughly reproduce the contents of my speech as follows:—

I began by expressing quite directly the feelings which gripped me, and could not but grip me, as I now saw the last member of our family called away. [Peter had lost his father, mother, three brothers and three sisters, and he alone was left.] All of them, with one exception had reached years of maturity.

But, I went on, I must not dwell on these things in these circumstances and in this company. There is indeed, I said, a good deal of public interest in our family, aroused by the personality and writings of the deceased. If it did not centre in the children, it certainly did in their father—that old man, the head of the family, who had stood by all his children's graves except the deceased here and my own.

[1] Peter's writing is exceedingly small. I have seen examples in the Royal Library in Copenhagen. (Translator.)

To give any assessment of my brother's activities adequate to so large an audience, was not to be thought of. One thing above all others is certain, namely that there were many there present, from all classes of society, who would confess that they owed to him a Christian awakening, or a further development in their appropriation of Christianity. Equally there were many others who, without being able to express it, had been impelled through him towards mighty emotions and conflicts in their spiritual lives. Finally, there were certainly many present who had learnt from him to regard as mere appearance and deception, nearly everything that has been presented as Christianity down the ages. Some even thought that Christianity was so exceedingly high a matter, as to be beyond their powers to practise, and therefore its challenge had no claim upon them.

With such a mixed audience, the speaker felt unable to say all he might have said to the different sections alone. Some among them regarded Søren as a John the Baptist warning us of the Lord's coming with winnowing fan to cleanse his floor; and warning us so forcibly that the very warning itself had acted like a winnowing fan. Others almost regarded Søren as a fallen Samson, who with his fall had overturned the Christian Church as established among the Danish people. The speaker might have ventured to speak to the various sections of his audience and to have hoped for sympathy and understanding from at least some of them, were he not so deeply affected by his brother's burial. But he *would* venture to say—and in this he knew he was in accord with the deceased, who had always been thankful for all the lessons and sufferings and activities of life—that for us and for a great part of the Danish Church, a challenge had been put. He thanked the All-Highest for allowing Søren Kierkegaard to witness and act among us as he did on behalf of truth and the reality of Eternity.

And here he would confess, on his own behalf and possibly on behalf of many others too, especially among the Danish clergy, that he felt a heart-felt shame and repentance because none of us had done anything for Søren in the strain and stress of his last years, when his blows fell as wildly as Ølver's in the Nordic myth. We ought to have done as Ølver's friends did. With love's sure vision we ought to have persuaded or forced him to take a period of rest and quiet recuperation, right away from all this overwhelming strain.

Accordingly, the speaker would end by praying to God the Father, in Jesus' name, that He would lead us by His Spirit to make a right use of all the forceful witness which Søren, whom God's will had now called from us, would have borne among us. We must not let ourselves be hindered by gazing upon what was wrong and misleading.

This, as Geismar says,[1] was a tactful and humble speech; and some of the newspaper reports quoted above similarly describe it. After all, here was a dead man who, under the *Corsair* attacks (as he himself had said in 1850), 'had affronted nobody, nobody. But unfortunately it is true that Denmark is a small country, and the *Corsair* represents public opinion. There is the rub. I did a good deed, absolutely, but people were led to think it a crime, because they thought I was setting myself against public opinion. To whom can I speak? Nobody. The majority have long ago sworn enmity against me. A few individuals understand me to a certain extent, but find the cost too heavy to say so. The literary élite rejoice at the misconception.'[2] But he had the courage, in spite of almost universal enmity, to run his life and carry out what he believed God's will, to the end.

Let me end this section by quoting some words from the *Aalborg Post* of 21 and 22 February 1886. They come in a report of a speech Peter Kierkegaard made against a certain fanatic named M. A. Sommer. 'Just as Søren', says Peter, 'sent me a brotherly greeting in his last days (though at second hand), in spite of the antagonism which our differing convictions gave rise to in the last years of his life, so I know that I am still one with him in his prayer upon his sick bed, for more light, for fearlessness in death, for forgiveness of sins and eternal salvation. Equally I know I am one with Søren in contending that Christianity is not doctrine but existence. Only I would have added that existence is life, and therefore must begin, germinate, grow and ripen. One must not lay the demands of maturity upon everyone who confesses the Christian faith, lest by such demands he should put him off from it.'

[1] Geismar, *Søren Kierkegaard* VI, p. 101.

[2] *Papirer*, X^3, A, 73.

VI. ABOUT REGINE SCHLEGEL

On 29 November 1855, Peter was at Søren's rooms in Klædeboderne (now Skindergade 38), to see to the disposition of his property. With him was Søren's secretary Israel Levin. Levin tells us (the document is in the Kierkegaard archive in the Royal Library), 'After Kierkegaard's death, everything in his room was found to be arranged as if he were going on a journey into the country. After some time a key was found. What did it belong to? It was to his desk. In the desk was a letter to Peter. There were present at the time Peter, Lynge the bookseller, and ——' (the cypher probably, as Weltzer suggests, *Peter and Søren Kierkegaard*, p. 275, represents Levin himself). 'Kierkegaard took the letter, read it, and was so deeply affected by it that he had to sit on a chair for a few minutes to collect himself. No-one knows what the letter contained.' There was another letter too. In his diary for Oct. and Nov. 1855 Peter writes 'In Søren's rooms received two letters to myself, 29/11'.[1] Of the first letter, Niels Thulstrup says 'it was presumably written in 1849, at the same time as the sketches of letters to Fr. and Regine Schlegel.[2] From the same period too comes the entry "My relationship to her."'[3] The first letter was sealed with black wax and reads:—

1

Testament

Dear brother,

> It is of course my will that my erstwhile fiancée, Mrs. Regine Schlegel, shall inherit unconditionally all the little I can leave. If she will not have it, it is at her disposal to give to the poor at her own discretion. What I wish to indicate is that an engagement is to me as binding as a marriage, and therefore my effects belong to her just exactly as if I had been married to her.

2

The other was sealed with red wax, and dated August 1851. It reads:—

> The one unnamed, whose name some day will be named—to whom all my work is dedicated, is my erstwhile fiancée, Mrs. Regine Schlegel.

[1] Both are printed in Raphael Meyer, *Forlovelsen*, p. 75 ff., and N. Thulstrup, *Breve og Aktstykke*, p. 25 (Commentary thereon, p. 14). Peter's diaries are in Copenhagen University Library, N.K.S. 3005.

[2] X^5, A, 148–150, partly translated in Dru's *Journals*, 367. See Thulstrup's Commentary, 14, 235.

On the envelope of both letters alike was written:—

To Pastor Dr. Kierkegaard.
To be opened after my death

Peter Kierkegaard let Hr. Schlegel and Regine know forthwith the contents of the 'testament'. Schlegel was by that time Governor of the Danish West Indies.[1] Peter received the following answer:—

3

St. Croix
14 January 1856

On New Year's Day I received your reverence's letter of 23 November ultimo, and I seize the opportunity to send you an answer by the first departing steamship.

First of all, may I, on behalf both of my wife and myself, thank you and your kinsfolk for the discretion you have observed in this matter; which for many reasons we should not have liked to see made a subject for gossip.

As regards the surprising news your letter contains, I have to say as follows: At first my wife was uncertain whether she was not bound by duty to fulfil the deceased's wishes in the way indicated by the second sentence of his letter [i.e. to distribute S.K.'s effects to the poor]. But she has now given up her qualms, partly because of the difficulty of distance, and partly because she and I do not see ourselves justified in accepting such a commission. It seems to be based on motives and view-points she cannot agree with. Your own private note to me made the deceased's meaning still clearer; and though I felt it my duty to leave the decision in my wife's hands, I did venture to acquaint her with what you said. She bids me therefore to ask you and your fellow-executors to go forward just as if this 'testament' had not existed. She would merely like to keep some letters and some small things to be found in the deceased's possession, which were formerly hers. She herself has written to Henrik Lund about these.

I have informed Hr. Maag the attorney direct about this decision of my wife.

With deepest respects
I remain,
Your reverence's respectful
F. Schlegel

Two letters from Regine to Henrik Lund may fittingly close this little book of glimpses at a bygone age. They both are replies to Henrik.

[1] See note at the end of section IV, p. 115. [2] Raphael Meyer, *Forlovelsen*, p. 142ff.

4

Whit Monday
12 May 1856

Dear Henrik,

He who was the cause of our becoming acquainted, and who is now the cause of our coming into correspondence with each other, once ascribed to you that very beautiful trait in a character—faithfulness. That was many years since. Whatever else the intervening years have taught me, I have learnt that that word was true of you. . . .

Thank you very much for fulfilling my wish. Two of the brooches were mine, and I am glad to receive them. The third I have not seen before, but to send it back from so great a distance is, as you rightly say, not worth the trouble. I will therefore keep it. The rings were right. That with the clear stone was changed to the form of a cross, not I think without significance. It saddens me however that I have perhaps deprived one of you of a precious memento. I think it was right that with God's help you sent me all the letters, both those destined to be burnt and others. For it was his wish that I should have everything, and he knew that of all his papers I should be specially careful to examine just these. And this I have done, with a humble prayer to God for His blessing; so I hope that good will accrue to me and not harm. Convinced that it will, I beg you to keep nothing back from me, whatever it be, whether in word or writing. I thought I understood that some of his writings, kept in a rosewood cabinet, were meant for me, but perhaps I was mistaken. That you 'according to orders' [from God] have sent me his surviving portrait was indeed absolutely right. God tempts no man, and if it were not His will that I should come to know what now I do know, this would not have happened. Although there has been no elucidation between us since he said Goodbye to me (an unopened letter you found, I agreed with my husband and my best conscience, to send back to him unopened), I expected some elucidation after his death, although I must confess not exactly in the form I have received it [i.e. the bequest of all his property to her together with his statement of fidelity]. . . .

5

The second letter is dated 10 September [1856].

Dear Henrik,

Please do not think that because I have let your letter of June 11 lie so long unanswered, I am therefore not grateful for it. On the contrary I have thanked you for it many times in my heart, and send you today my thanks in words. It is always my rule to answer letters by return of post, but every rule has its exception and so I made your letter one. We two anyhow do not carry on a regular correspondence, so a little pause means nothing; and moreover, there is a request I want to put to you, and something I want to say to you which I wanted to consider carefully. I have been out of sorts lately too. I do not stand the very hot weather well; it weakens my nerves. But I have been having boils, which is a very healthy sign out here; and so I am the better able to write letters. You say you almost regret you did not come to St. Jean. . . . [At this point the letter becomes broken and incoherent. But Søllerød is mentioned, and the reader will recall that Troels-Lund tells us (see section IV above, *ad finem*), that Henrik paid a visit to the West Indies, and that his father got him a house at Søllerød after his return.] Thank you for the books you send me. If it is not too much trouble and sacrifice for you, I would ask you, if you have not already sent them, for some of his theological writings. Some I have, especially the latest.

That was the request I wanted to make to you. Now for my question. You say he mentioned me when he lay ill. I did so much want to know what he said about me.[1] For a new light has come on our relationship from his Posthumous Papers [which Peter and you have sent me.] I have indeed sometimes seen things in such a light myself; and yet (I do not know if you will understand me if I say this), while my modesty forbade me to see things thus, my unshakeable faith in him constantly brought me back to believing it were so. You see I was uncertain; and yet what I did feel certain about was that there was some unsettled point between us which one day must be cleared up. And I short-sightedly put off the clarification till the quiet time of old age. With astonishing thoughtlessness, it never occurred to me that he might die. His death therefore came the more unexpectedly upon me, and filled me not only with sorrow but with repentance; as though by thus postponing clarification I had done him a great wrong. It was this I wanted to be clear about, by hearing what his last words about me were; for his Papers, so far as I can understand, were all written many years back; and the years have brought great changes with them. Among the papers, I found a sealed one whereon it merely said 'It is my will that my writings be dedicated to my deceased father and her.' Strangely enough, that dedication 'To an unnamed', which stands at the beginning of a little volume of three Discourses, I have always understood to refer to me, since the day I first saw it. Can you elucidate for me whether I am right? His purpose in that case was to bestow on me joy and honour such as pertained to his own famous name; and to a large extent I can be happy because I have received both joy and honour in such a high measure, that it is as if the whole world shares this with me, though in fact no-one shares it with me. I have always shrunk from openness; and out here, where I am so public a figure, I feel this all the more. Keeping quiet therefore has cost me absolutely nothing. But things look different now he is dead. I feel I have shirked a duty through cowardice; a duty not only towards him but towards God to whom he sacrificed me—whether he did this (as he himself sometimes thought *might* be the case) through an inborn tendency to self-torture, or, as I take it that time and the results of his activities have shown, through an inner call from God. Any enlightenment you can give me will not change my attitude, as you will understand, towards my husband and his position. But I do feel a desire to get things clear to myself as far as possible so I will no longer put off the matter in silence. I have done enough of that in my life.

[1] What he actually said on his deathbed about Regine, as reported by Pastor Boesen who visited him was, 'I have my thorn in the flesh like Paul. Hence I could not be like other folk, so I concluded that my task was to be the extraordinary. . . . It was this that was the hindrance with R.; I had believed it could be changed, but it could not. So I broke the engagement.' *E.P.* IX, p. 593.

I have still something else to reveal to you. (Notice how immodestly I assume your deep interest for me by laying bare to my secret qualms. But I know I can rely on you, can I not?) You say that you think you can detect from my letter that I am not exactly happy. This you can perhaps rightly deduce from the letter you then received; for you know by experience how much we mortals are the victims of feelings. But I should be very ungrateful if I did not call myself fortunate, yes fortunate as few are. For as is so often said, 'a happy marriage is life's greatest blessing'. And Schlegel and I are so much to each other that we mutually enrich each other's lives. In a way I owe this to him also. . . .

[Here the letter breaks off as we have it.]